T0384947

An Analysis of

Aristotle's

Politics

Katherine Berrisford
with
Riley Quinn

Published by Macat International Ltd
24:13 Coda Centre, 189 Munster Road, London SW6 6AW.

Distributed exclusively by Routledge
2 Park Square, Milton Park, Abingdon, Oxon OX14 4RN
711 Third Avenue, New York, NY 10017, USA

Routledge is an imprint of the Taylor & Francis Group, an informa business

www.macat.com
info@macat.com

Cataloguing in Publication Data
A catalogue record for this book is available from the British Library.
Library of Congress Cataloguing-in-Publication Data is available upon request.
Cover illustration: Etienne Gilfillan

ISBN 978-1-912303-17-5 (hardback)
ISBN 978-1-912128-37-2 (paperback)
ISBN 978-1-912282-05-0 (e-book)

Notice
The information in this book is designed to orientate readers of the work under analysis,
to elucidate and contextualise its key ideas and themes, and to aid in the development
of critical thinking skills. It is not meant to be used, nor should it be used, as a
substitute for original thinking or in place of original writing or research. References and
notes are provided for informational purposes and their presence does not constitute
endorsement of the information or opinions therein. This book is presented solely for
educational purposes. It is sold on the understanding that the publisher is not engaged
to provide any scholarly advice. The publisher has made every effort to ensure that
this book is accurate and up-to-date, but makes no warranties or representations with
regard to the completeness or reliability of the information it contains. The information
and the opinions provided herein are not guaranteed or warranted to produce particular
results and may not be suitable for students of every ability. The publisher shall not be
liable for any loss, damage or disruption arising from any errors or omissions, or from
the use of this book, including, but not limited to, special, incidental, consequential or
other damages caused, or alleged to have been caused, directly or indirectly, by the
information contained within.

CONTENTS

THE MACAT LIBRARY

The Macat Library is a series of unique academic explorations of seminal works in the humanities and social sciences – books and papers that have had a significant and widely recognised impact on their disciplines. It has been created to serve as much more than just a summary of what lies between the covers of a great book. It illuminates and explores the influences on, ideas of, and impact of that book. Our goal is to offer a learning resource that encourages critical thinking and fosters a better, deeper understanding of important ideas.

Each publication is divided into three Sections: Influences, Ideas, and Impact. Each Section has four Modules. These explore every important facet of the work, and the responses to it.

This Section-Module structure makes a Macat Library book easy to use, but it has another important feature. Because each Macat book is written to the same format, it is possible (and encouraged!) to cross-reference multiple Macat books along the same lines of inquiry or research. This allows the reader to open up interesting interdisciplinary pathways.

To further aid your reading, lists of glossary terms and people mentioned are included at the end of this book (these are indicated by an asterisk [*] throughout) – as well as a list of works cited.

Macat has worked with the University of Cambridge to identify the elements of critical thinking and understand the ways in which six different skills combine to enable effective thinking.
Three allow us to fully understand a problem; three more give us the tools to solve it. Together, these six skills make up the **PACIER** model of critical thinking. They are:

ANALYSIS – understanding how an argument is built
EVALUATION – exploring the strengths and weaknesses of an argument
INTERPRETATION – understanding issues of meaning

CREATIVE THINKING – coming up with new ideas and fresh connections
PROBLEM-SOLVING – producing strong solutions
REASONING – creating strong arguments

To find out more, visit **WWW.MACAT.COM.**

CRITICAL THINKING AND *POLITICS*

Primary critical thinking skill: PROBLEM-SOLVING
Secondary critical thinking skill: EVALUATION

Aristotle remains one of the most celebrated thinkers of all time in large part thanks to his incisive critical thinking skills. In *Politics,* which can be considered one of the foundational books of the western political tradition, the focus is on problem-solving, and particularly on the generation and evaluation of alternative possibilities.

Aristotle's aim, in *Politics*, is to determine how best to organize a society. He looks in turn at several different type of organization – kingship, oligarchy and the polity, or rule in the hands of many – and evaluates the arguments for each in turn. But he takes the exercise further than his predecessors had done. Having concluded that rule by the aristocracy would be preferable, since it would mean rule by citizens capable of taking decisions on behalf of the society as a whole, Aristotle subjects his solution to a further checking process, asking productive questions in order to make a sound decision between alternatives.

Politics was ground-breaking in its approach. Unlike previous thinkers, Aristotle based all his ideas on a practical assessment of how they would play out in the real world. Ultimately, Aristotle argues, the problem of self-interest means that the adoption of a mixed constitution – one based on carefully considered laws which aims at a balance of power between the people and the elite – is most likely to bring eudaemonia (happiness). It's a conclusion firmly based on careful evaluation (not least the process of judging the adequacy of arguments) and the product of outstanding problem-solving skills.

ABOUT THE AUTHOR OF THE ORIGINAL WORK

Aristotle was born in 384 B.C.E. in what is present-day Macedonia. At the age of 17 he moved to Athens in Greece to begin an education in philosophy under Plato, one of the founders of European philosophy, at his renowned Academy. On Plato's death in 347 B.C.E., Aristotle moved back to Macedonia to tutor the young Alexander the Great. But in 335 B.C.E. he returned to Athens and established his own school, the Lyceum. Political unrest forced Aristotle to leave Athens again in 322 B.C.E., and he died shortly afterwards on the island of Euboea.

ABOUT THE AUTHORS OF THE ANALYSIS

Katherine Berrisford is researching a PhD thesis in political theory at the University of Exeter.

Riley Quinn holds master's degrees in politics and international relations from both LSE and the University of Oxford.

ABOUT MACAT

GREAT WORKS FOR CRITICAL THINKING

Macat is focused on making the ideas of the world's great thinkers accessible and comprehensible to everybody, everywhere, in ways that promote the development of enhanced critical thinking skills.

It works with leading academics from the world's top universities to produce new analyses that focus on the ideas and the impact of the most influential works ever written across a wide variety of academic disciplines. Each of the works that sit at the heart of its growing library is an enduring example of great thinking. But by setting them in context – and looking at the influences that shaped their authors, as well as the responses they provoked – Macat encourages readers to look at these classics and game-changers with fresh eyes. Readers learn to think, engage and challenge their ideas, rather than simply accepting them.

'Macat offers an amazing first-of-its-kind tool for interdisciplinary learning and research. Its focus on works that transformed their disciplines and its rigorous approach, drawing on the world's leading experts and educational institutions, opens up a world-class education to anyone.'

Andreas Schleicher
Director for Education and Skills, Organisation for Economic Co-operation and Development

'Macat is taking on some of the major challenges in university education ... They have drawn together a strong team of active academics who are producing teaching materials that are novel in the breadth of their approach.'

Prof Lord Broers,
former Vice-Chancellor of the University of Cambridge

'The Macat vision is exceptionally exciting. It focuses upon new modes of learning which analyse and explain seminal texts which have profoundly influenced world thinking and so social and economic development. It promotes the kind of critical thinking which is essential for any society and economy.
This is the learning of the future.'

Rt Hon Charles Clarke, former UK Secretary of State for Education

'The Macat analyses provide immediate access to the critical conversation surrounding the books that have shaped their respective discipline, which will make them an invaluable resource to all of those, students and teachers, working in the field.'

Professor William Tronzo, University of California at San Diego

WAYS IN TO THE TEXT

KEY POINTS

- Aristotle (384–322 B.C.E.) was an ancient Greek philosopher.
- In his text *Politics*, believed to have been written between 335 B.C.E. and 323 B.C.E., he argues that political communities create the necessary conditions in which mankind can flourish.
- Aristotle's ideas remain persuasive today.

Who Was Aristotle?

Aristotle, the author of *Politics*, was a philosopher. He was born in 384 B.C.E. in Stagira, a city in the Kingdom of Macedonia in the northeastern part of the Greek peninsula. At the age of 17, he went to Athens, the center of learning in the classical Greek world, to study with the philosopher Plato*—whom many people considered to be the greatest thinker in the Western tradition. Aristotle remained a student at Plato's Academy* until 348 B.C.E.

In 343 B.C.E., he returned to Macedonia to become the personal tutor of the young Alexander the Great,* a man who would later conquer vast territories in Mediterranean Europe, including Greece, North Africa, and Asia.

The political structure of Greece underwent dramatic changes during these years. For centuries, the *polis*—the small city-state and its surrounding territories—had dominated Greek political life. But the Macedonian rulers had begun to build an empire that would eventually stretch from southeast Europe all the way to what today is India.

In 335 B.C.E., the year after Alexander became the king of Macedonia, Aristotle returned to Athens. He established his own school, The Lyceum,* named after the public meeting place where lessons were held. There, he lectured his students on subjects that included politics, physics, poetics, and logic. But the death of Alexander the Great in 323 B.C.E. brought renewed political instability. Popular opinion in Athens turned against the Macedonians. Aristotle's connection with Macedonia was well known, and he was forced into exile, dying in 322 B.C.E.

Yet Aristotle's legacy certainly endures. Well over 2000 years later, his ideas continue to remain relevant.

What Does *Politics* Say?

In *Politics*, Aristotle says that living in a politically organized community of citizens sharing similar goals can make people better human beings. By "better," he means more virtuous: more fair, more just, and more generous. Aristotle also argues that possessing these virtues makes people happier. So, he says, living in close association with other people is a "natural" behavior, because it has the capacity to make us happier.

But what is the best way to organize a society?

In *Politics,* Aristotle describes three ways in which societies are organized: 1) power in the hands of one person (kingship), 2) power in the hands of a small group (an oligarchy),* and 3) rule in the hands of the many (a polity).* He discusses the theoretical arguments for each of these forms of rule and looks at real-world examples, concluding that the best form of government would be rule by an aristocracy:* a small group of the "best" citizens, who would make decisions in the best interests of society as a whole.

Aristotle says, however, that this form is unlikely to work successfully in the real world because most people make decisions that further their own interests rather than the community interest. As a result, he concludes, the best form of government would be a "mixed constitution."*

For Aristotle, "constitution" refers to the laws determining who holds power within a society. In a mixed constitution, he notes in *Politics,* power is balanced between the many and the elite. Each group limits the other's power, allowing decisions to be made that benefit the whole community. Aristotle emphasizes the importance of the law. The ultimate purpose of any community is to bring happiness ("eudaemonia"*) to its citizens, so the laws that governed the *polis* would have to be written carefully to ensure they furthered that goal. Aristotle says that although people cannot be relied on to behave in a way that furthers community happiness, carefully considered laws can help prompt them to behave in a virtuous way.

He also highlights the importance of education in *Politics*. If the state educated its future citizens, teaching them to share in its values, those values would be maintained.

Politics was groundbreaking in its approach. Unlike previous thinkers, Aristotle based all his ideas on a practical assessment of how they would play out in the real world. In the book, he examines how real-world factors can lead a constitution into decline. A kingship can degenerate into a tyranny.* An aristocracy can degenerate into an oligarchy. A polity can degenerate into a democracy* (that is, rule by the public—far from Aristotle's favored system).

Aristotle argues that the key factor that makes a constitution degenerate is imbalance. For example, a society with too many poor people relative to the number of rich people, with a negligible middle class, will naturally become a democracy. Or, when the rich are too powerful in relation to the other classes, a society will naturally become an oligarchy.

The problem with degenerate societies is that they create factionalism,* which occurs when a single group becomes too powerful. Society then becomes organized in a way that serves the interests of that group, rather than the interests of the community as a whole. And factionalism leads to revolutions, which destroy the state.

Aristotle concludes that societies are most likely to achieve happiness if middle classes dominate them. Being neither very poor nor very rich, these societies are unlikely to degenerate into factionalism.

Why Does *Politics* Matter?

It is thanks to *Politics* that Aristotle has become known as the world's first political scientist. His predecessors had tried to imagine ideal or imaginary forms of things like justice or society. In contrast, Aristotle's work focuses on actual city-states. He asks how real people practicing politics in the real world can create political communities that support, serve, and improve their citizens. This approach, based on the analysis of observable information, is known as "empiricism"* and has been a feature of political science ever since.

Aristotle's thinking has had a profound influence on thinkers throughout history. His famous statement that "man is a political animal" has ongoing implications for the way societies are organized. He meant that it is natural for people to live within political communities and to share common goals.

In the European Middle Ages* (the period of about a thousand years following the fall of the Roman Empire), people regarded Aristotle as a source of truth about politics. The scholars of the day analyzed his works line by line, as they sought to understand all his ideas. In the twentieth century, he inspired a political philosophy based on the *good* that a government can achieve. This was in contrast to modern liberal* thought, according to which, government should not interfere in the lives of its citizens.

Aristotle argued that society existed to benefit both the rich and the poor. As a result, his political thought led to a rejection of the politics of imbalance and exclusion. This argument remains vitally important today. It has helped define the Capability Approach* to economic development, according to which, economic development should not just make developing countries richer but should also enable the people in those countries to pursue a good life. This is one of the most important theories in the field of development economics today.

Aristotle's ideas have also helped to define modern attitudes to distributive justice*—a consideration of the ways in which goods should best be shared out within a society. Thinkers inspired by Aristotle argue that the goods should go to those who can best realize their worth. In other words, the best flutes should go to the best flute players, for example, because the virtue of flutes is to produce beautiful music.

Politics was groundbreaking. Despite the changes in the world that have occurred since Aristotle conceived his ideas, its concepts are still relevant now. Aristotle inspired political thinkers throughout history. As a result, to understand the history of political thought, it is vital to understand Aristotle.

SECTION 1
INFLUENCES

MODULE 1
THE AUTHOR AND THE HISTORICAL CONTEXT

KEY POINTS

- Aristotle's *Politics* is relevant because it was the first work of political science.

- Aristotle was born in ancient Greece. He spent most of his life in Athens, first as a student of the enormously influential Greek philosopher Plato* and then running his own school.

- Athens was a *polis**—a small community composed of a city and its surrounding territories. The government of the *polis* was entrusted to citizens who worked for the good of the whole community.

Why Read This Text?

Aristotle's *Politics* is believed to have been written between 335 B.C.E. and 323 B.C.E. It is famous for being the first work to deal with politics as a science. Unlike earlier thinkers, Aristotle based his ideas on evidence. The philosopher Plato, Aristotle's teacher, focused on an ideal, theoretical, political community. In contrast, Aristotle was interested in how human societies could best function in the real world.

In the text, Aristotle describes how the natural condition of humanity is to live in the *polis*, the community dwelling in the city and the city's environs. "Man is by nature a political animal," he thinks.[1] For him, the needs of survival create the initial impetus for forming a community. But Aristotle also believes that living in a *polis* or political community can make its citizens happier and more virtuous.

> ❝ He never seems to have doubted that being Greek and living in a small *polis* was the supreme form of human existence, nor that the study of the polis was worth the investment of huge intellectual resources over a long period. ❞
>
> Malcolm Schofield, "Aristotle: An Introduction"

By "virtue,"* Aristotle means possessing excellence of character. One key aspect of this is a person's ability to manage his impulses. To eat moderately, for example, is virtuous because it shows an individual can manage his appetite. Living close to, and exchanging views with, other people encourages individuals to become more virtuous. And living virtuously—within an environment that supports virtuous living—makes people happy.

In the twentieth century, virtue ethicists* revived this belief that the political community is the source of human happiness. These thinkers introduced the concept that human happiness is based on developing good qualities—justice, generosity, and so forth. This belief, in turn, inspired the Capability Approach* to economic development of the 1980s, which held that economic development should improve the life chances of those it affects and help them to develop the qualities that will make them happier.

Author's Life

Aristotle was born in Stagira, in what is now northeastern Greece, in 384 B.C.E. His father Nicomachus, a notable physician, died when Aristotle was a child. By the time Aristotle was 17, his mother, Phaestis, had also died. Aristotle's guardian, a friend of his parents, "handed over the young man to Plato"—who was already a significant figure in the world of philosophy. Aristotle was sent to Athens to study philosophy at Plato's Academy*[2] where he stayed for the next 20 years—first as a student and then as a teacher—only leaving after Plato's death in 347 B.C.E.

Many of the Athenian students at the academy viewed their education as training for a life spent in the practice of politics. Aristotle did not. He threw himself into philosophical education for its own sake, devoting "the rest of his life to philosophical discussions and to a way of life dedicated to the cultivation of the intellectual virtues."[3] Aristotle's status as a metic* may have partly influenced that. "Metic" was the Athenian term for a resident foreigner. Although often well-respected members of the community, metics were excluded from participating in political life and forced to pay special taxes.

After Plato's death, King Philip II* of Macedon hired Aristotle to tutor his son Alexander, who would later become known, after conquering huge swathes of the ancient world, as Alexander the Great.* This connection with Philip, Alexander, and Macedonia would affect the rest of Aristotle's life.

At 50, Aristotle returned to Athens and founded his own school, The Lyceum.* It flourished, but after 13 years, conflict broke out between the Athenians and the Macedonians. Aristotle had expressed support for Macedonian rule. As a result, the Athenians forced him into exile. He died soon after.

Author's Background

Aristotle lived at the end of the Classical period* of Greek history, a time defined by the flowering of art and philosophy. The *polis** dominated the political life in Classical Greece. *Polites* (pronounced "polities"), the plural of *polis*, were city-states that ruled over a city and its surrounding territories. Stagira, Aristotle's birthplace, was a *polis*. So was Athens, where Aristotle lived and worked for most of his life. He never doubted that "living in a small *polis* was the supreme form of human existence," worth protection and reflection.[4]

"Aristotle's *Politics*," writes the British historian Paul Cartledge,*
was "based on research into more than 150 of over 1,000 separate and
jealously independent Greek polites." These city-states ringed the
Mediterranean and stretched into Asia Minor (modern Turkey).[5] But
they were not all ruled in the same way. Democracy* and oligarchy*
(rule by a small group of people) "were the two most widespread
forms of constitution."*[6]

Aristotle uses "constitution" in *Politics* to refer to the laws deciding
in whose hands power should be led: one of the work's key themes.

Democracy in Aristotle's time would not be recognizable to the
modern voter. A democratic *polis* "was a strong community of adult
male citizens with defined honors and obligations." Anyone who was
not an adult male citizen was a second-class member of society and
was denied the privilege of the vote.[7] Male citizens had the right (and
obligation) to participate in democratic citizen assemblies and also had
the obligation (and privilege) to join military campaigns against other
city-states.

In Aristotle's time, however, this model of the city-state was in
decline. The rise of Macedon under Philip II and Alexander the Great
threatened to bring Greece together under a single ruler. One by one
the Macedonians conquered the Greek city-states and incorporated
them into their Hellenistic Empire.* The once-powerful citizen
assemblies became little more than town councils. Alexander died in
323 B.C.E. But his conquests—stretching across the known world,
from Italy to India—spelled the end of the Classical era.

Aristotle died a year after Alexander, just as the Hellenistic Age*—
the period between the Classical age and the Roman period, when
Greek cultural influence was at its peak—was beginning.

NOTES

1   Aristotle, *Politics*, 70. Book III, Chapter 6, in *The Politics and The Constitution of Athens*, ed. Stephen Everson of *Cambridge Texts in the History of Political Thought*, series editors Raymond Geuss and Quentin Skinner (Cambridge: Cambridge University Press, 1996), $1278^b/19$–20.

2   Carlo Natali, *Aristotle: His Life and School* (Princeton: Princeton University Press, 2013), 11.

3   Natali, *Aristotle*, 19.

4   Malcolm Schofield, "Aristotle: An Introduction," in *The Cambridge History of Greek and Roman Political Thought*, ed. Christopher Rowe et al (Cambridge: Cambridge University Press, 2000), 317.

5   Paul Cartledge, "Greek Political Thought: The Historical Context," in *The Cambridge History of Greek and Roman Political Thought,* ed. Christopher Rowe et al (Cambridge: Cambridge University Press, 2000), 21.

6   Cartledge, "Greek Political Thought," 21.

7   Cartledge, "Greek Political Thought," 17.

MODULE 2
ACADEMIC CONTEXT

KEY POINTS

- "Politics" means "things of the city." Political philosophy explores the ways in which people relate to political communities.

- Socrates*—the enormously influential philosopher who taught Aristotle's teacher, Plato—was interested in the true nature of virtues, such as justice. Aristotle was more interested in how virtues could be supported in the real world.

- Pre-Socratic* philosophers, or the philosophers who preceded Socrates, saw philosophy as an inquiry into the natural world. They were less interested in studying human politics than Aristotle was.

The Work in its Context

Aristotle's book *Politics* is concerned with the concept of "constitutions":* the laws determining who holds power within a society.

Writing about the Ancient Greeks, the British historian Paul Cartledge* argues that "for both practical and theoretical reasons they enriched or supplemented politics with practical ethics." In other words, the Greek conception of politics was that *political participation is in itself a good thing*.[1] "Ancient thinkers," writes the political philosopher Ryan Balot,* "believed that the *polis* should provide for the ethical and emotional education, character development, and appropriate religious participation of its citizens" and that political life and personal life were bound up in one another to an enormous degree.[2]

❝ Mortals suppose that gods are born, wear their own clothes and have a voice and body. ❞
Xenophanes, *Fragments*

Given that political structures and personal lives were so entwined, the over-riding concern of political philosophy in ancient Greece was to find the ideal constitution. A city could be ruled as a monarchy* (by a king), as an aristocracy* (by a small group of particularly appropriate people), or the polity* (the citizens as a whole). In other words, the constitution could place power in the hands of one person, a few people, or everyone.

In *Politics,* Aristotle argues that the ideal community would be based on an aristocracy, by which he means the best, most suitable people, tasked with governing in the interests of the whole community. He says, however, that this is unlikely to happen; rulers tend to rule for their own sake, rather than for the sake of others.

Overview of the Field
Aristotle was writing in two traditions of Greek philosophy: the Pre-Socratic* tradition and the Platonic* tradition.

The British scholar A. A. Long* says that the pre-Socratic philosophers were interested in "giving an account of all things." To discover the true nature of things, they studied nature, rather than myths.[3] Their interests were closer to what is now called science, rather than what is now called philosophy. At the time they were working, however, the distinction between these two ways of thinking was not clearly defined.

One of the most famous pre-Socratic philosophers, Xenophanes,* criticized Greek religion, the followers of which believed in a group of gods called the Olympians* because they lived on Mount Olympus.

He argued that the Greeks invented the gods in their own image:"But if … horses … had hands then horses would portray their gods as horses."[4] Xenophanes believed there was a single, underlying "force" or "one god" that was shared by all things—from human beings, to wind, to trees.

Unlike the pre-Socratics, Socrates did not philosophize about the natural world, but about ethics. He did not write anything himself; others, notably his student, Plato,* wrote about him. Plato wrote several Socratic dialogues, prose works in which characters (usually including Socrates himself) discuss moral problems.

Like the pre-Socratics, Socrates wanted to discover the true nature of things. His concern was to find true justice. In Plato's dialogue *Gorgias*, Socrates says:"I believe that I'm one of a few Athenians … to take up the true political craft and practice the true politics. This is because the speeches I make on each occasion do not aim at gratification but at what's best."[5] Plato shows that Socrates wanted politics to fulfill its primary function: to improve the lives of those in the *polis*.

Academic Influences

Although Aristotle's most important influence was Plato (and, through Plato, Socrates), his study of the pre-Socratics also influenced his thinking. He believed these "inquirers into nature" were doing a very important job, yet he disagreed with their methods.

The pre-Socratics focused on the "true nature" of things, rather than looking at what things did. To a pre-Socratic, rain falling from the sky "is really nothing more than the coincidental behavior of the objects that constitute the nature of reality."[6] They were not interested in why rain fell from the sky or in the effect that it had on other things when it did so.

In contrast, Aristotle was concerned with the way things behaved. In his work *Physics*, he outlines "four causes" that he believes determine the way in which the world functions. The most important is Aristotle's "final cause": the reason why a given object exists. The acorn's *final cause*, for example, is to become an oak tree.[7] In other words, while the pre-Socratics were primarily concerned with speculating on the material of the world, Aristotle was concerned with action in the world.

Like Socrates, he was interested in questions that relate to humanity. But while Socrates examined the nature of virtues such as wisdom and justice, Aristotle examined how these qualities could be supported within human societies.

NOTES

1   Paul Cartledge, "Greek Political Thought: The Historical Context," in *The Cambridge History of Greek and Roman Political Thought*, ed. Christopher Rowe et al (Cambridge: Cambridge University Press, 2000), 12.

2   Ryan Balot, *Greek Political Thought* (Oxford: Blackwell, 2006), 4.

3   A.A. Long, "The Scope of Early Greek Philosophy," in *The Cambridge Companion to Early Greek Philosophy* (Cambridge: Cambridge University Press, 1999), 10.

4   David Sacks, "Xenophanes," In *A Dictionary of the Ancient Greek World*. Oxford (Oxford University Press, 1995), 267.

5   Plato, *Gorgias*, trans. Robin Waterfield (Oxford: Oxford World's Classics, 1995), 521d6–9.

6   Thomas Blackson, *Ancient Greek Philosophy* (Chichester: Wiley-Blackwell, 2011), ebook.

7   Aristotle, *Physics*, trans. Robin Waterfield (Oxford; Oxford World's Classics, 2008), Book V, Chapter 1, 1031a.

MODULE 3
THE PROBLEM

KEY POINTS

- A key concern for the philosophers of Ancient Greece was to answer the question, "Which is the best way of organizing society?"
- Plato wrote about a "utopia"*—that is, an impossible paradise.
- Instead of theorizing about an unachievable paradise, Aristotle used evidence to assess different ways of organizing society.

Core Question

In his book *Politics,* Aristotle, like Plato, asks the question, "What is the best method of organizing society?" To organize society effectively, it is important to know what that society wants to achieve.

In the final section of another of his famous works, the *Nicomachean Ethics*, Aristotle had written about the relationship between politics and individual goodness: "The end of politics is the best of ends; and the main concern of politics is to engender a certain character in the citizens and to make them good and disposed to perform noble actions."[1]

This idea that politics exists to improve man appears to be common among Greek thinkers. The method by which humanity is to be improved is through laws, or in Aristotle's words, "It is through laws that we can become good."[2]

In *Politics*, Aristotle argues that if men become good by living in law-abiding societies, then the primary task of the philosopher is to work out which laws should be in place—believing that politics is the art of improving humanity through making laws that support ethical

> ** Now our predecessors have left the subject of legislation to us unexamined; it is perhaps best, therefore, that we should ourselves study it, and in general study the question of the constitution, in order to complete to the best of our ability the philosophy of human nature. **
>
> Aristotle, *Nicomachean Ethics*

behavior. This is not the same as being a statesman. Dorothea Frede,* a professor of philosophy at the University of California, says that "Aristotle attributes to the laws not only the supreme authority in education, but also the respective executive power."[3] In other words, Aristotle believes that a state's constitution (its form of government and its laws) is the most powerful force shaping its citizens. The constitution is the key to the good life.

The Participants

Aristotle's teacher Plato, in his most famous work, *The Republic*, had posed the question "What is the nature of justice?" Plato wrote *The Republic* as a Socratic dialogue between Socrates and various other characters. In it, Plato argues that "justice" is only found in a city with a perfect constitution. Plato imagines a perfectly just city, which he calls "Callipolis* (roughly, "Beautiful City").

In Callipolis, Plato theorizes, all property (including wives and children) would be held in common, and the sexes would have equality in the military. These arrangements were so unusual that Plato believed such a society could only come about if "philosophers rule as kings" or if existing kings become philosophers.[4] But Plato argues that if any city did enforce all of his unusual laws it would be a kind of utopia—an imaginary place of perfect justice.

There is still debate about Plato's intentions in describing

Callipolis. Some scholars believe that he meant Callipolis to be a blueprint for a real city of perfect justice. Others argue that his description was simply intended to provoke interest in the argument. In either case, Plato is making a case for a philosopher king* as an idealized form of benevolent tyranny.

The Contemporary Debate

Influenced by Plato above all others, Aristotle's *Politics* raises some of the same questions as Plato's *Republic*. Both books ask, "What is the perfect constitution for the rule of a city?" Plato's aim was "to consider what form of political community is best of all for those who are most able to realize their idea of life."[5] This goal is related to Aristotle's main goal: to understand which constitution best supports people in living ethically.

Aristotle also takes on some of Plato's key ideas. "Don't you know," says one of Socrates' debating partners in *The Republic*, "some cities are ruled tyrannically,* some democratically,* and some aristocratically?"[6]

Aristotle uses similar categories in *Politics*. In fact, he responds directly to one idea that Plato puts forward in *The Republic*. In Book II of his *Politics*, he dismisses the idea that all property should be shared in common.[7] But this helps to show that Plato shaped Aristotle's project. Indeed, the aspects of Platonic thought that Aristotle chose to reject are as important as the ideas he shared.

The British philosopher of the mind Stephen Everson* argues that Aristotle rejects Plato's version of the perfect constitution because of Plato's "unguarded enthusiasm for theorizing."[8] Plato's tendency to dream up answers to his questions out of thin air is "as likely to take one away from the truth as it is to help one to attain it." Aristotle keeps his theory much more grounded. His objective is to consider how his theory would work in the real world, rather than in the realm of pure philosophy.[9]

NOTES

1   Aristotle, "Nicomachean Ethics: Book X, Chapter 9," in *The Politics and The Constitution of Athens*, ed. Stephen Everson of *Cambridge Texts in the History of Political Thought*, series editors Raymond Geuss and Quentin Skinner (Cambridge: Cambridge University Press, 1996), 3-7 1099^b/30.

2   Aristotle, "Nicomachean Ethics," 3-7, 1180^b/25–27.

3   Dorothea Frede, "The Political Character of Aristotle's Ethics," in *The Cambridge Companion to Aristotle's Politics* (Cambridge: Cambridge University Press, 2013), 16.

4   Plato, *The Republic*, ed. G.R.F. Ferrarri, in *Cambridge Texts in the History of Political Thought* series editors Raymond Geuss and Quentin Skinner (Cambridge: Cambridge University Press, 2003), 472e.

5   Aristotle, *Politics*, 30–31. Book II, Chapter 1, in *The Politics and The Constitution of Athens*, ed. Stephen Everson of *Cambridge Texts in the History of Political Thought*, series editors Raymond Geuss and Quentin Skinner (Cambridge: Cambridge University Press, 1996), 1270^b/27–28

6   Plato, *The Republic*, 338d.

7   Aristotle, *Politics*, 31–32. Book II, Chapter 2. 1271^a /10.

8   Stephen Everson, "Introduction," in *The Politics and The Constitution of Athens*, ed. Stephen Everson, *Cambridge Texts in the History of Political Thought*, series editors Raymond Geuss and Quentin Skinner (Cambridge: Cambridge University Press, 1996), xiii.

9   Everson, "Introduction," xiii.

MODULE 4
THE AUTHOR'S CONTRIBUTION

KEY POINTS

- Aristotle believed humanity could achieve happiness through political association—that is, through living in communities with a political organization. He thought the way to find this kind of political association lay in studying constitutions.*
- Before Aristotle, "pure idealism" dominated political philosophy—not the study of the real world.
- *Politics* logically follows Aristotle's work *Ethics*, in which he developed his theory that political association enables the development of virtue.

Author's Aims

In *Politics*, Aristotle evaluates and studies different constitutions, aiming to identify which one best enables people to live well. In another work, *Nicomachean Ethics*, Aristotle wrote that "our predecessors have left the subject of legislation to us unexamined; it is perhaps best therefore to study the question of the constitution, in order to complete to the best of our ability the philosophy of human nature."[1] Aristotle carried out this investigation into the constitution in *Politics*.

It is worth noting that *Politics* is thought to be a collection of Aristotle's lecture notes.[2] Scholars who accept this theory believe that *Politics* formed the basis of the lectures that he delivered to his students at his school, The Lyceum,* an "important center of secondary education in Athens"[3] where Aristotle trained the future leaders of Athens and other city-states.

Given his audience, it is not surprising that Aristotle chose to emphasize the study of real political constitutions, more or less

> ❝ So, do you think that our discussion will be any less satisfactory if we cannot demonstrate that it is possible to found a city that is the same as the one we described in speech? ❞
>
> Plato, *The Republic*

abandoning the mode of utopian thought associated with his teacher Plato.* Aristotle was not training future philosophers; he was training future politicians and generals. The fact that *Politics* probably represents a collection of lecture notes, rather than a book that Aristotle intended to publish, also has implications for the way the work is written.

Approach

Aristotle's aim in *Politics* is "to consider what form of political community is best of all."[4] Like his predecessors, he shared the belief that man was made good or better by living in societies governed by laws. Previous thinkers—Plato among them—theorized about "perfect states." These states did not exist; this was pure philosophy, with the objective of imagining what could be. In the text, Aristotle examines previous theories about the perfect state, but also looks at "other constitutions … such as actually exist in well-governed states."[5] In other words, Aristotle's method is more scientific—he works from the evidence to discover which constitution is the most beneficial for its citizens.

In this new approach to political philosophy, Aristotle abandons the theoretical search for an "ideal" way of doing things in favor of looking at how people can create stable political communities that benefit their citizens. He uses evidence to defend his approach. Addressing Plato's argument that all property ought to be equalized, Aristotle turns to history, citing the tale of a ruler who experimented with the edict that "the citizens of the state ought to have equal possessions."

Aristotle shows that this edict led to many men having more property than they were accustomed to, resulting in citizens "living in luxury or penury," which, in turn, caused political unrest.[6] Aristotle assesses the merit of the claim that people should have equal property on the basis of the evidence, rather than through abstract theory.

Contribution in Context

To grasp *Politics* fully, it is essential to understand the final chapters of Aristotle's work, *Nicomachean Ethics*. This was the text that first depicted humankind achieving happiness—*eudaemonia**—through the correct combination of nature, habit, and excellence.[7] According to Aristotle, people may have a deep-rooted need to be virtuous, but to realize that need they also have to practice virtuous behavior and live in an environment that supports and reinforces virtuous behavior. People who make laws "ought to stimulate men to excellence and urge them forward by the motive of the noble," he says. In other words, because most men will not choose by themselves to be noble, the state—which has laws that exist to help improve mankind—should force them to be better.[8]

Many scholars believe that the final section of the *Nicomachean Ethics* shows Aristotle making a transition from thinking about ethics to thinking about politics. There is a logical connection between *Politics* and *Ethics* because

Aristotle asserts that man can become virtuous (the object of ethics), through political community and the right constitution. At the end of *Ethics,* Aristotle writes, "When [constitutions] have been studied we shall perhaps be more likely to see which constitution is best, and how each must be ordered and what laws and customs it must use."[9] This is "practical wisdom": it considers ethical issues and the *effect* of those ethical considerations. That combination of theory and practical experience was innovative, shaping the tradition of political theory.

NOTES

1   Aristotle, "Nicomachean Ethics," 7. Book X, Chapter 9, in *The Politics and The Constitution of Athens*, ed. Stephen Everson of *Cambridge Texts in the History of Political Thought*, series editors Raymond Geuss and Quentin Skinner (Cambridge: Cambridge University Press, 1996), 1181^b/11–15

2   Stephen Everson, "Introduction," in *The Politics and The Constitution of Athens*, ed. Stephen Everson, *Cambridge Texts in the History of Political Thought*, series editors Raymond Geuss and Quentin Skinner (Cambridge: Cambridge University Press, 1996) x/xi.

3   John Patrick Lynch, *Aristotle's School: A Study of a Greek Educational Institution* (Berkeley: University of California Press, 1972), 46.

4   Aristotle, *Politics*, 30. Book II, Chapter 1, in *The Politics and The Constitution of Athens*, ed. Stephen Everson of *Cambridge Texts in the History of Political Thought*, series editors Raymond Geuss and Quentin Skinner (Cambridge: Cambridge University Press, 1996), 1260b/25–31.

5   Aristotle, *Politics*, 30. Book II, Chapter 1, 1260b/25–31.

6   Aristotle, *Politics*, 43-46. Book II, Chapter 7, 1266b/1–40.

7   Aristotle, *Politics*, 184-185. Book VII, Chapter 13, 1332^a/8 -1332^b/10.

8   Aristotle, "Nicomachean Ethics," 3-7. Book X, Chapter 9, 1180a/7–8.

9   Aristotle, "Nicomachean Ethics," 3-7. Book X, Chapter 9, 1181b/20–23.

SECTION 2
IDEAS

MODULE 5
MAIN IDEAS

KEY POINTS

- Aristotle said that man's natural state is living within a political society.
- He argued that political association helps people to become just and work towards their common interest.
- Scholars are still debating the way *Politics* is structured.

Key Themes

In *Politics* Aristotle has three key themes:

- Teleology.* *Telos* means "end" and, according to the principle of teleology, everything is defined by its end state. For example, a seed is defined by its purpose to become a plant. Every political community also comes together to accomplish a particular end.
- The "good life." Aristotle discusses what this is and how it might be achieved.
- The constitution* of the political community (or, roughly, the laws deciding how power is distributed). Aristotle assesses the different forms a constitution might take and which form best serves its citizens.

These three key themes fit together to produce Aristotle's overall argument: man's ultimate purpose is to become more virtuous through living within a political community. This is what he means by the famous phrase, "man is by nature a political animal."[1] A person's "natural state" is living in association with other human beings, and

> ❝ Every state is a community of some kind, and every community is established with a view to some good; for everyone always acts in order to obtain that which they think good. But, if all communities aim at some good, the state or political community, which is the highest of all, and which embraces all the rest, aims at good in a greater degree than any other, and at the highest good. ❞
>
> Aristotle, *Politics*

humanity can find happiness living in the political community. Therefore, Aristotle argues, it is natural that political communities form, and it is ethically right that a community's laws ensure the improvement of its citizens.

Aristotle discusses three different types of constitutions in *Politics*: rule by the one, rule by the few, or rule by the many. He says that each of these constitutions has a true form and a "perverted" form. When the rulers of a community aim to provide for the *polis** as a whole, then the constitution is true. When the rulers seek only their own private good, the constitution is perverted. The good constitutions are kingship (the one), aristocracy (the few), and constitutional polity (the many). The bad constitutions are tyranny (the one), oligarchy (the few), and democracy (the many). This is not an original distinction, Aristotle points out, but one Plato made that he expanded.[2]

Exploring the Ideas

Aristotle introduces the concept of teleology right at the start of *Politics*, writing: "Every state is a community of some kind, and every community is established with a view to some good."[3] Aristotle gives a swift account of how political communities emerge: they begin with "natural" couplings of man and woman, master and slave, and children in "households." Several households join so that they can fulfill the "bare needs of life" more effectively.[4] As more households come together, forming a larger society, the "bare needs" of life are more than adequately fulfilled. At this point, the households continue to associate "for the sake of the good life."[5]

But what is the "good life" according to Aristotle?

It is not only that humans find satisfaction from being together, he says, but, through sharing opinions with others, people develop concepts of good and bad, justice and injustice.[6] Aristotle believes that politics, goodness, and justice are all products of human nature and human intelligence, realized through our capacity to speak to one another about our ideas. He argues, "Political society exists for the sake of noble actions." By "noble actions," Aristotle means the pursuit of justice—working together to achieve "the common interest."[7]

Politics is the means by which the "common interest" is determined. Aristotle says that social goods should be distributed in a way that favors the good of the citizens as a whole, rather than, for example, those with wealth.[8] He gives the example of a flute player, arguing that the best flute player should be given the best flute on the basis of his ability to play the flute. Politics is a mechanism by which man can incentivize people to work towards the common interest.

Language and Expression

Students of politics must keep several issues in mind when reading *Politics*.

First, *Politics* is not a stand-alone work. Aristotle's discusses much of his understanding of the good life and *telos* in *Nicomachean Ethics*, and the two texts are closely related. Second, most scholars believe that Aristotle did not write *Politics* for publication. The American political scientist Carnes Lord* says that the most common assumption about Aristotle's works is that they "represent notes which served as the basis for lectures given by Aristotle to students of The Lyceum."[9]

The German classicist Werner Jaeger,* a famous scholar of Aristotle, believed that *Politics* was not even a coherent set of lecture notes. He argued that the books that make up *Politics* were cobbled together at a later date, because books IV to VI deal with Aristotle's practical notions of government in the real world, while other books (I to III and VII to VIII) are much more idea-driven.[10]

Lord disagrees with Jaeger. He thinks it is possible that *Politics* was not a set of lecture notes, but rather a reference work given to students. In this interpretation, the internal inconsistencies in the work come from student annotations and transcription errors, which would be "difficult to distinguish from earlier additions by Aristotle himself."[11] The organization and method of *Politics* is still under debate.

NOTES

1   Aristotle, *Politics*, 70. Book III, Chapter 6, in *The Politics and The Constitution of Athens*, ed. Stephen Everson of *Cambridge Texts in the History of Political Thought*, series editors Raymond Geuss and Quentin Skinner (Cambridge: Cambridge University Press, 1996), $1278^b/19$–20.

2   Aristotle, *Politics*, 93. Book IV, Chapter 2, $1289^b/45$–46.

3   Aristotle, *Politics*, 11. Book I, Chapter 1, $1252^a/1$–2.

4   Aristotle, *Politics*, 12. Book I, Chapter 1, $1252^b/30$.

5   Aristotle, *Politics*, 12. Book I, Chapter 1, $1252^b/31$.

6   Aristotle, *Politics*, 14. Book I, Chapter 1, $1253^a/10$-15.

7   Aristotle, *Politics*, 76. Book III Chapter 9, $1281^b/18$.

8   Aristotle, *Politics*, 80. Book III Chapter 12, $1282^a/39$–40.

9   Carnes Lord, "The Character and Composition of Aristotle's *Politics*," *Political Theory* 9, No. 4 (1981): 461.

10 Werner Jaeger, *Aristotle: Fundamentals of the History of His Development*, trans. Richard Robinson, (Oxford: Oxford University Press, 1948), 283-285.

11 Lord, "The Character and Composition of Aristotle's *Politics*," 474.

MODULE 6
SECONDARY IDEAS

KEY POINTS

- According to Aristotle, a constitution* based on the middle class—meaning a state governed by the middle class—has the most realistic chance of making citizens more virtuous.

- Factionalism,* or splits in the community, along lines of wealth leads to the degeneration of the constitution of a state.

- Aristotle argues that public, universal education will help safeguard a constitution.

Other Ideas

In *Politics*, Aristotle explains why political life is important and describes how communities should be organized. "We should consider not only what form of government is best," he writes, "but also what is possible and what is easily attainable by all."[1]

How does a *polis* make improvements in the way it is organized and governed? Aristotle devotes Books IV to VIII of *Politics* to explaining how his political theories can be applied in the real world.

To comprehend Aristotle's arguments, it is vital to understand the difference between politics as an *episteme* (or a "science,") and politics as a *techne* (or "art.") In this context, "art" does not refer to a cultural form such as a painting, but rather to a trade such as carpentry or masonry. According to the British academic Stephen Everson* in his introduction to a collection of Aristotle's writings, "In possessing an art someone is capable of producing something: a doctor can produce health because he possesses the art of medicine." So, for Aristotle, "The political scientist can produce states."[2]

> **"** The best is often unattainable, and therefore the true legislator and statesman ought to be acquainted, not only with which is best in the abstract, but also with that which is best relatively to circumstances. **"**
>
> Aristotle, *Politics*

Aristotle's main ideas look at the theory of what makes a good state. His secondary ideas look at how those theories may be translated into the production of real states: the art of politics.

Exploring the Ideas

"What is the best constitution for most states," Aristotle asks in *Politics*, "and the best life for most men?"

He asks this question in the context of conditions that actually exist in the real world.[3] One of the factors he considers is the social mix within a city in which "one class is very rich, another very poor, and a third in [the middle]."[4] The percentage of the population that falls into each class will make each city-state very different from another. They will then have different constitutions. "Where the number of the poor exceeds a given proportion, there will naturally be a democracy," Aristotle writes, and when the wealthy gain a disproportionate amount of power, there will be an oligarchy.[5]

A disproportionate number of either poor or rich is deeply problematic, he continues. In this situation, the rich will become greedy, and the poor will become petty. Factions* will form in which people at the extremes of society develop a distorted view of justice. From factions come revolutions and the destruction of the state.

According to Aristotle, to prevent the social distortions that occur when people seek to further their own desires and advantages above all else, the best constitution should be organized around the middle classes "for no other is free from faction." Without factions, the political community is better able to unite around the common interest.[6] The middle classes also have a balanced view of justice. They do not "covet other men's goods; or do others covet theirs." This class is able to both command and obey, but does not resent being commanded.[7]

Aristotle's ideas about a constitution based on the middle classes is neither an oligarchy* (a government ruled by a small and wealthy elite), nor a democracy* (a government led by all adult men eligible to debate and vote). It is a *polity*,* a mix between these two forms of government.

Aristotle's belief that, in the real world, the middle way is best, is prevalent throughout the book.

Overlooked

One aspect of *Politics* that scholars have often overlooked is Aristotle's discussion of education. Aristotle presents an argument for state education in Book VIII of *Politics*.[8] It is necessary for rulers to educate children, he argues, so that they learn the skills and virtues required to maintain a sound constitution. Since "the whole city has one [purpose]," he writes, "it is manifest that education should be one and the same for all, and that it should be public and not private."[9]

In the ideal society, according to Aristotle, the state would provide equal access to education to the children of all citizens. He claims that there is an important link between education and the character of the state, since "the character of democracy creates democracy, and the character of oligarchy creates oligarchy; and always the better the character, the better the government."[10] So the state can cultivate the character of its future generations by investing in their education. This system could be viewed as a means of indoctrination, ensuring that citizens do not resist the power of the state. It could also be viewed as an egalitarian and liberating proposal that guarantees a certain level of education for the state's citizens.

Recent scholars have highlighted Aristotle's discussion of education, arguing that it represents an important part of his overall thesis.[11] The Belgian academic Pierre Destrée* points out that education helps people to flourish within the state by teaching them the values of the state: "It is because we are 'political animals,' that is animals who need to live in a city in order to fulfill their desire for happiness by sharing in some values and in activities that express those values, that the way to be prepared for such a life must be provided by the city we live in."[12]

NOTES

1   Aristotle, *Politics*, 92. Book IV, Chapter 1, in *The Politics and The Constitution of Athens*, ed. Stephen Everson of *Cambridge Texts in the History of Political Thought*, series editors Raymond Geuss and Quentin Skinner (Cambridge: Cambridge University Press, 1996), 1288^b/36–38.

2   Stephen Everson, "Introduction" in *The Politics and The Constitution of Athens*, ed. Stephen Everson, *Cambridge Texts in the History of Political Thought*, series editors Raymond Geuss and Quentin Skinner (Cambridge: Cambridge University Press, 1996).

3   Aristotle, *Politics*, 92. Book IV, Chapter 1, 1294^b/25–27.

4   Aristotle, *Politics*, 107. Book IV, Chapter 11, 1295^b/1–22.

5   Aristotle, *Politics*, 109. Book IV, Chapter 12, 1296^b/24–27.

6   Aristotle, *Politics*, 108. Book IV, Chapter 11, 1296^a/7.

7   Aristotle, *Politics*, 108, Book IV, Chapter 11, 1295^b/29–30.

8   Aristotle, *Politics*, 195-207. Book VIII.

9   Aristotle, *Politics*, 195. Book VIII, Chapter 1, 1337^a/21–23.

10 Aristotle, *Politics*, 195. Book VIII, Chapter 1, 1337^a/16–18.

11 Pierre Destrée, "Education, Leisure and Politics" in *The Cambridge Companion to* Aristotle's *Politics*, eds. Marguerite Deslauriers and Pierre Destrée (Cambridge and New York: Cambridge University Press, 2013), 301–323.

12 Destrée, "Education", 306.

ACHIEVEMENT

KEY POINTS

- Although Aristotle's *Politics* has inspired many political thinkers, people have criticized it because he does not offer details about how to realize all his ideas.
- Aristotle was a prominent teacher and intellectual in Athens.
- Aristotle's argument for "natural slavery" has made some modern readers uncomfortable with the work. However, other interpreters believe Aristotle was actually condemning slavery.

Assessing the Argument

In *Politics,* Aristotle presents his vision of the best possible political structure within the constraints of the real world. His intention was to work out how people could be improved by life within the community—and in some ways, he achieves this. Aristotle articulates a number of core points: what the aim of a society should be, what kinds of societies there are, and which kind of society is best at improving the lives of its citizens.

However, some thinkers believe *Politics* is an unfinished work. Aristotle's explanation of how the state is to be arranged lacks a detailed description of one important element: the education system.

Dorothea Frede,* a professor of philosophy at the University of California, notes that Aristotle's "plan for the citizen's education unfortunately is not carried out beyond the blueprint for the musical education of children."[1] Frede suggests two possible explanations for this. It is possible that certain aspects of a more complete work were lost. Aristotle could also have decided not to carry out a project of such size. It would be a nearly, it not totally, impossible task to list all of the factors that make for a successful education system.

❝ Aristotle's theory of natural slavery is at least potentially a critical theory. A slave owner who pondered it seriously would have to ask himself: 'Is my slave really a natural slave? Or is he too shrewd and purposeful?' ❞

Malcolm Schofield, "Ideology and Philosophy in Aristotle's Theory of Slavery"

Achievement in Context

If, as is widely believed, Aristotle's work *Politics* was created from reconstructed lectures that he delivered at his school, The Lyceum,* that indicates the impact Aristotle's teaching had during his lifetime. It is unlikely that his lecture notes would have been retained if he had not been intellectually influential.

The Peripatetic ("walking") scholars, named perhaps for Aristotle's style of pacing around as he taught, preserved Aristotle's work. The Lyceum and the peripatetic tradition remained important after Aristotle's death, as his students continued his work. The American historian David C. Lindberg* describes how, on Aristotle's death, Theophrastus,* a close associate of the philosopher "assumed the headship of The Lyceum."[2]

Although Theophrastus continued Aristotle's program of research, his only surviving works focus on botany and geology. The texts in the library of The Lyceum, including Aristotle's writings, were bequeathed to notable scholars around the Mediterranean, eventually ending up in the hands of the Greek philosopher Andronicus of Rhodes* who "arranged and edited them, bringing them into prominence and wider circulation."[3] In the twelfth century, William of Moerbeke,* a Flemish philosopher and monk from what today is the Netherlands, translated *Politics* into Latin. That brought Aristotle's ideas to a wider audience, which recognized their significance immediately.

Although many aspects of Aristotle's wider philosophy aroused mistrust in the Roman Catholic Church, the intellectual tradition known as Scholasticism*—which was concerned with collecting, preserving and using the wisdom of the past—helped to reconcile Aristotelian thought with Catholic doctrine.

Limitations

One key aspect of Aristotle's *Politics* has been particularly off-putting to modern readers: his defense of the institution of slavery and his idea that some people are "natural slaves." According to Aristotle, "that which can foresee by the exercise of mind is by nature lord and master," and he who can carry out what his master foresees is "by nature a slave."[4]

Aristotle believes this arrangement is mutually beneficial since masters and slaves share the same goals. However, the "natural master" cannot carry out all his plans on his own, and the "natural slave" is not capable of independent planning—he has to be directed to act. Aristotle does, however, argue against slavery by "convention." He says that the practice in which a rational human being is made a slave simply because he or she has had the misfortune of being captured should not be allowed.[5] This is not a mutually beneficial relationship.

Some scholars, notably the British classicist Malcolm Schofield,* believe that Aristotle may have been subtly making a case *against* slavery. Schofield points out that, in criticizing slavery "by convention" (through capturing people) Aristotle argues that the vast majority of humanity should be excluded from slavery. After all, how many people are incapable of thought? Schofield suggests that Aristotle may have written his chapters on slavery to force "a slave owner [to] ask himself: 'Is my slave really a natural slave? Or is he too shrewd and purposeful?'"[6] So it is important to interpret Aristotle's ideas about slavery carefully. It may be that they contain an implicit criticism of the "unethical" practice of the slavery common at Aristotle's time.

NOTES

1   Dorothea Frede, "The Political Character of Aristotle's Ethics," in *The Cambridge Companion to Aristotle's Politics* (Cambridge: Cambridge University Press, 2013), 33.

2   David C. Lindberg, *The Beginnings of Western Science: The European Scientific Tradition in Philosophical, Religious, and Institutional Context, Prehistory to AD 1450* (Chicago: University of Chicago, 2008), 73.

3   Lindberg, *The Beginnings of Western Science*, 74.

4   Aristotle, *Politics*, 12. Book 1, Chapter 1 in *The Politics and The Constitution of Athens*, ed. Stephen Everson of *Cambridge Texts in the History of Political Thought*, series editors Raymond Geuss and Quentin Skinner (Cambridge: Cambridge University Press, 1996), 1252^a/31–34.

5   Aristotle, *Politics*, 19. Book 1, Chapter 7, 1255^b/12–14.

6   Malcolm Schofield, "Ideology and Philosophy in Aristotle's Theory of Slavery," in *Aristotle's Politics: Critical Essays*, ed. Richard Kraut and Steven Skultety (Lanham: Rowman and Littlefield, 2005), 100.

MODULE 8
PLACE IN THE AUTHOR'S WORK

KEY POINTS

- Some thinkers argue that *Politics* was composed at two different times since the early books are more "Platonist" (more obviously bearing the influence of Aristotle's teacher Plato) than the middle books.

- Aristotle used the same analytical approach to every subject he wrote about. He would break down the basic principles of an art or science in order to find its core meaning.

- Aristotle also wrote across many disciplines, including poetics, physics, and natural science. His work in all these disciplines has been extremely influential.

Positioning

Different sections of Aristotle's *Politics* may have been composed at the different times. As a result, it is hard to assess what position this work holds in relation to Aristotle's other writing.

Aristotle wrote his early work while he was still under the influence of the ideas of his teacher Plato.* These pieces contain more Platonic concepts than Aristotle's later work. The British academic Thomas Case* explained Plato's doctrine as viewing all existence as reflecting perfect, supernatural "forms." So tables are only "tables" because they resemble the "ideal form" of a perfect, theoretical table.

Aristotle, in contrast, holds that all things are separate. Tables are not all reflections of a perfect, supernatural table. They are understood to be tables because they possess individual qualities that make them more table-like than chair-like.[1] Some thinkers—notably the German classicist Werner Jaeger*—have concluded that Aristotle began his

> ❝ *Politics* is to be ranked amongst the greatest works of political philosophy. ❞
>
> Stephen Everson, "Introduction," in *Politics*

intellectual life as a Platonist* but became more "Aristotelian" as he developed into a more established thinker in his own right.[2]

Some of the books that make up *Politics* offer a Platonic theory of political ideals (books I to III and books VII to VIII), while others display an Aristotelian commitment to the study of individual constitutions (books IV to VI). Scholars still debate whether Aristotle wrote *Politics* early or late in his career, or whether the book straddles both periods of his life.

Integration

Aristotle's intellectual life was not focused purely on politics; he was a broad-ranging scholar who inquired into logic, science, rhetoric,* and even poetry. Aristotle's approach to these subjects, however, was consistently analytical and methodical; he broke down whatever he was studying into its fundamental parts. He then used this knowledge of the fundamental building blocks of a discipline to study how it emerged and the best way that it could develop.

Aristotle opens his *Poetics*, for example: "We are to discuss both poetry in general and the capacity of each of its genres; the canons of plot construction needed for poetic excellence; also the number and character of poetry's components ... beginning, as is natural, from first principles."[3] He seeks to understand the distinct parts of poetry, what makes poetry excellent, and how poetry can become excellent.

His investigation into animals proceeds in a similarly analytical way. "Of the parts of animals some are simple: to wit, all such as divide into parts uniform with themselves, as flesh unto flesh," he writes.

Others divide into distinct parts so that "the hand does not divide into hands nor the face into faces."[4] Aristotle breaks the complexity of animal life down into parts: hands are made of palms, fingers, and below this, cells. This methodical approach is thought of as distinctively Aristotelian.

Significance

"*Politics*," writes the British academic Stephen Everson,* "is to be ranked amongst the greatest works of political philosophy."[5] Yet Aristotle's other works also had a seminal influence on different disciplines. For example, his ideas about physics dominated Western science until the seventeenth century. And the Italian historian Stefano Perfetti* describes how Aristotle's work on zoology* was admired during the medieval period. "Halfway through the thirteenth century, we already find the entire corpus of Aristotle's natural writings" prescribed to students at the University of Padua, in what is now northern Italy.[6]

Although later scholarship superseded some of Aristotle's concepts, this is not necessarily true of *Politics*. Readers now criticize some sections of this work, such as its problematic sections on natural slavery and the role of women in society. But the core message of Aristotle's *Politics* remains at the heart of a flourishing contemporary political theory: that political affiliation can improve peoples' lives.

In the modern world, Aristotle has become a source of wisdom for a range of famous scholars including the Indian economist and Nobel laureate Amartya Sen,* the American philosopher Martha Nussbaum,* and even the American political philosopher Michael Sandel,* who is famous for his theories about justice and community.

NOTES

1   Thomas Case, "Aristotle," *Aristotle's Philosophical Development: Problems and Prospects*, ed. William Robert Wians (London: Rowman and Littlefield, 1990), 1–2.

2   Daniel Graham, *Aristotle's Two Systems* (Oxford: Oxford University Press, 1990), 5.

3   Aristotle, *Poetics*, 1, Book 1, translated by Richard Janko (Indianapolis: Hackett Publishing, 1987), 47^a/1-2.

4   Aristotle, *History of the Animals*, (Adelaide: University of Adelaide), ebook. https://ebooks.adelaide.edu.au/a/aristotle/history/book1.html

5   Stephen Everson, "Introduction" in *The Politics and The Constitution of Athens*, ed. Stephen Everson, *Cambridge Texts in the History of Political Thought*, series editors Raymond Geuss and Quentin Skinner (Cambridge: Cambridge University Press, 1996), 1.

6   Stefano Perfetti, *Aristotle's Zoology and its Renaissance Commentators* (Leuven: Leuven University Press, 2000), 1.

SECTION 3
IMPACT

MODULE 9
THE FIRST RESPONSES

KEY POINTS

- The earliest criticisms of *Politics* focused on Aristotle's overly careful, formal approach.
- *Politics* was treated as an authoritative source of political fact through the European Middle Ages* (roughly the fifth to the fifteenth century) and numerous scholars composed commentaries on it.
- By the early modern period,* which began around the end of the fifteenth century, scholars were less willing to accept Aristotle as authoritative. While they shared his interests, they wanted to gather their own evidence.

Criticism

Aristotle's *Politics* was probably not printed for wide distribution. As a result, people did not respond to it in any serious way until much later.

When Western thinkers rediscovered *Politics* in the thirteenth century, it had "far reaching consequences for political thought."[1] But although Aristotle's ideas inspired many Christian medieval scholars, *Politics* also provoked some criticism.

The Italian humanist* scholar Petrarch,* for example, argued that Aristotle's approach to politics is too careful and systematic. He took issue with Aristotle's notion that men can become noble simply by understanding what nobility is, rather than by being passionate about virtue. For Petrarch, political life is an emotional process; Aristotle was too calm.

"Aristotle explains what virtue* is," he writes, "but reading his works does not offer … words that set on fire the heart and make it

> 66 Let them keep their exorbitant opinion of every-
> thing that regards them, and the naked name Aristotle
> which delights many ignorant people by its four syllables.
> Moreover, let them have the vain joy and the unfounded
> elation which is so near to ruin; in short, let them have all
> the profit people who are ignorant and puffed up earn
> from their errors in vague and easy credulity. 99
> Petrarch, *On His Own Ignorance*

love virtue and detest vice."[2] Petrarch recognized the importance of
Aristotle's thought, however. He considered himself obliged to find a
position that reconciled the worldly and rational Aristotelian idea of
the "good life" with the Christian idea that a life should be valued by
the nature of our relationship to the divine.

Whereas Aristotle described "the good life" in terms of human
fulfillment in the world, for Petrarch, life without love for a personal
God—an idea connected to emotion and joy—could not be perfectly
described as "good."

Other thinkers, among them the Italian intellectual St Thomas
Aquinas,* resolved this by arguing that wisdom could be found in
many places. The key for Aquinas was to harvest that wisdom through
study.

Responses

The earliest comprehensive criticism of *Politics* that we have was
produced around a thousand years after Aristotle's death. He was,
therefore, unable to respond to it. Many thinkers appreciated, rather
than criticized, Aristotle's ideas. When his work was rediscovered in
the medieval period, scholars updated *Politics*, adapting it to the new
political structures of the day. This was a tacit way of showing
admiration for Aristotle's work, despite the fact that he "was without

the light of Christian revelation, and without the medieval conception of the church in society."[3]

In the medieval period, a movement called Scholasticism* dominated western intellectual thought. The aim of Scholasticism was to understand, and benefit from, all accessible sources of wisdom—rediscovered classical texts and the Bible alike. This movement arose in large part due to the desire of medieval scholars to reconcile Aristotelian thought with Catholic doctrine. Prominent thinkers in the Scholastic tradition, notably Aquinas, published commentaries on Aristotle's *Politics*—going through the text line by line to reveal the philosopher's insights.[4]

Aquinas's most famous work is *Summa Theologica*, which discusses the teachings of the Roman Catholic Church. Its primary goal was to unite worldly concerns like politics with issues of theology.* Aquinas cites Aristotle in *Summa,* despite the fact that Aristotle was not a Christian. Aquinas respectfully refers to Aristotle as "the Philosopher" and endorses many of his ideas. Quoting Aristotle's *Ethics*, for example, Aquinas writes: "The Philosopher says happiness is an operation according to perfect virtue."[5] Moreover, Aquinas argued, "The proper effect of the law is to lead its subjects to their proper virtue,"* thereby improving the character of those who obey the law.[6]

Conflict and Consensus

By the early modern period, attitudes towards Aristotle had begun to change. Although thinkers still considered his ideas inspirational, they were starting to use his methods to draw their own conclusions about the world. Writing about the early modern period, the British academic Ernest Barker* discussed the impact of Aristotelian thought on Niccolò Machiavelli,* a Florentine diplomat and political theorist who has been called the inventor of modern political theory and who was, says Barker, "nurtured upon Aristotle from birth."[7] According to Barker, Machiavelli used Aristotle's classification of constitutions: rule by one, rule by the few, or rule by many.

Both thinkers were interested in understanding how tyrants preserve their power. Writing of tyranny—the "perverted" form of kingship—Aristotle says, "Though power must be retained as the foundation in all else the tyrant should act or appear to act in the character of a king." In other words, the tyrant should appear to act as a ruler who cares for the common interests of his subjects.[8] Those words mirror Machiavelli's famous advice that "a ruler who succeeds in creating [a generous] image of himself will enjoy a fine reputation."[9]

However, Barker also argues that Machiavelli "cannot be said to be indebted to Aristotle." Unlike the medieval commentators, "he does not lay down general principles from Aristotle" as though they are authoritative, but rather "collects the facts of the present" and draws his own conclusions.[10] Moreover, Machiavelli rejects the link between morality and politics. Aristotle believed that the ultimate end of politics was to improve the lives of citizens. For Machiavelli, politics was just a way of achieving power. Aristotle rejected Plato's* idealism in favor of greater empiricism.* In the same way, Machiavelli rejected Aristotle.

NOTES

1   Christopher Kleinherz, ed., "Aristotle and Aristotelianism," *Medieval Italy: An Encyclopedia*, (Oxford: Routledge, 2004), 56.

2   Petrarch, quoted in Christopher Kleinhenz, *Medieval Italy: An Encyclopedia Volume I A-K* (Oxford: Routledge, 2004), 117.

3   Conor Martin, "Some Medieval Commentaries on Aristotle's *Politics*," *History* 36 (1951): 34.

4   St. Thomas Aquinas, *Commentary on Aristotle's Politics*, translated by Richard J. Regan (Indianapolis: Hackett), 2007.

5   St. Thomas Aquinas, *Summa Theologica*, (Mobilereference: 2010), 1867.

6   Aquinas, *Summa Theologica*, 3108.

7   Sir Ernest Barker, *The Political Thought of Plato and Aristotle* (New York: Dover Publications, 1959), 515.

8 Aristotle, *Politics*, 148. Book 5, Chapter 11 in *The Politics and The Constitution of Athens*, ed. Stephen Everson of *Cambridge Texts in the History of Political Thought*, series editors Raymond Geuss and Quentin Skinner (Cambridge: Cambridge University Press, 1996), $1314^a/39$–40.

9 Niccolò Machiavelli, *The Prince*, ed. Quentin Skinner and Russell Price (Cambridge: Cambridge University Press, 1988), 63.

10 Barker, *The Political Thought of Plato and Aristotle*, 517.

MODULE 10
THE EVOLVING DEBATE

KEY POINTS

- One of Aristotle's key ideas was called political naturalism:*
  the idea that it is natural for humans to live in the *polis*.*
  This aspect of his thought was reinvigorated in the eighteenth
  century by thinkers like the conservative Irish statesman
  Edmund Burke.*

- *Politics* inspired the modern school of thought known as
  virtue ethics.*

- The American philosopher Martha Nussbaum* applies virtue
  ethics to politics. She suggests that political communities
  should aim to develop the virtues of their citizens.

Uses and Problems

Aristotle's *Politics* had an enormous effect on medieval political
philosophy. The Scottish philosopher J. H. Burns* writes, "The
translation of Aristotle's *Politics* and *Nicomachean Ethics* was crucial" for
the political thought of the thirteenth century.[1]

By the early modern period,* political thinking had changed.
Aristotle believed that politics could lift the citizens of a *polis* out of
"mere life," helping them to achieve "the good life." But during the
early modern period,* from around the sixteenth to the eighteenth
centuries, the political philosophy known as liberalism* started to gain
influence. Grounded in ideas about individual freedom and equality,
liberalism argued that the role of the state was to enable individual
liberty, rather than to improve its citizens. The English political
philosopher Thomas Hobbes* famously criticized *Politics* for just this
reason, saying, "Scarce anything can be … more repugnant to

> 66 If I recollect rightly, Aristotle observes that a democracy has many striking points of resemblance with a tyranny. Of this I am certain, that in a democracy, the majority of the citizens is capable of exercising the most cruel oppressions upon the minority. 99
>
> Edmund Burke, *Reflections on the Revolution in France*

government than much of that he hath said in *Politics*."[2] Hobbes believed that the state existed to provide—exclusively—for the "mere life" of its citizens.

Liberalism,* however, had its critics, who shared some of Aristotle's ideas. In 1791, the Irish statesman Edmund Burke wrote his now-famous *Reflections on the Revolution in France*. In it, he criticized the liberal ideas that underpinned the democratic French Revolution,* noting, "Aristotle observes … that a democracy has many striking points of resemblance with a tyranny."[3] Burke also shared Aristotle's belief that political association, with power distributed properly, will ultimately improve all those who participate in it. "Whenever man is put over men, as the better nature ought ever to preside, in that case more particularly, he should as nearly as possible be approximated to his perfection."[4]

Schools of Thought

Today, Aristotle's ethical and political thought is one of the key inspirations for virtue ethics, a movement in philosophy concerned with the moral principles governing an individual's actions. Other approaches to ethics include deontology,* which is concerned with the rules an individual follows and consequentialism,* which focuses on the consequences of an individual's actions.

The field of virtue ethics emphasizes the virtues. If there were a debate as to whether a drowning person should be saved, then "a virtue ethicist will emphasize the fact that helping the person would be charitable or benevolent."[5] They would also argue that it is good—virtuous—for people to be charitable or benevolent.

The British philosopher G. E. M. Anscombe* was one of the discipline's most important thinkers. Her article "Modern Moral Philosophy," first published in 1958, helped to embed modern virtue ethics as a distinctive line of inquiry.[6] Anscombe and the other virtue ethicists are primarily interested in Aristotle's *Ethics* rather than *Politics*. They use the idea of acting virtuously (developing oneself) as an alternative to acting "morally" (following the instructions of a lawmaker). Anscombe argued that ethical actions are ethical not because they follow some set of given *rules*, but instead because they are in accordance with a set of *virtues*.

In Current Scholarship

Virtue ethics can be applied to real-world politics. Referring to ethical theories too abstract to be useful in the real world, the American philosopher Martha Nussbaum* writes, "From many different sides one hears of a disaffection with ethical theories that are remote from concrete human experience."

One of the first to apply virtue ethics to modern political theory, Nussbaum goes on to say that Aristotle "was not only the defender of an ethical theory based on the virtues, but also the defender of a single objective account of the human good."[7] Some thinkers claim that what is good varies from person to person. Nussbaum argues that Aristotle believed in a state of being that was beneficial to all human beings—"the good life"—which people could achieve by developing their virtues. Aristotle also described the virtues that they needed to develop, providing an ethical guide to human existence that can be applied in the real world. His ideas can be used to improve key areas of human endeavor like education or law-making.

Nussbaum herself provides "a sketch for an objective human morality based upon the idea of virtuous action—that is, of appropriate functioning in each human sphere."[8] In other words, she presents an overview of ethics based on an objective idea of what is good for humanity, such as the development of virtues like courage, kindness, and generosity.

NOTES

1   J.H. Burns, "Introduction: Politics, Institutions, and Ideas," in *The Cambridge History of Medieval Political Thought* (Cambridge: Cambridge University Press, 1988), 356.

2   Thomas Hobbes, *Leviathan*, ed. J.C.A. Gaskin (Oxford: Oxford University Press, 1998), 143, 445.

3   Edmund Burke, *Reflections on the Revolution in France* (New Haven: Yale University Press, 2003), 106.

4   Burke, *Reflections*, 79.

5   Rosalind Hursthouse, *On Virtue Ethics* (Oxford: Oxford University Press, 1999), 1.

6   G. E. M. Anscombe, "Modern Moral Philosophy," *Philosophy* 33, No. 124 (1958), 1–19.

7   Martha Nussbaum, "Non-Relative Virtues: An Aristotelian Approach," *Midwest Studies in Philosophy XIII* (1988), 33.

8   Nussbaum, "Non-Relative Virtues," 39.

MODULE 11
IMPACT AND INFLUENCE TODAY

KEY POINTS

- Aristotle is honored today as the founder of political science as a distinct discipline.
- The idea that political communities ought to improve the lives of those who live in them has become central to the capability approach* to development, according to which "development" should mean more than simply an increase in a country's income.
- Some thinkers believe the "capabilities" developed by the capability approach are too "Western." They say that it is not possible to make objective lists of virtues.

Position

The German American political philosopher Leo Strauss* highlighted the importance of Aristotle's *Politics* in the modern world, writing: "Aristotle is truly the founder of political science."[1] Aristotle was among the first thinkers to study politics by considering real-world examples and applications rather than pure ideas alone.

In her book *A Democracy of Distinction: Aristotle and the Work of Politics*, the American political scientist Jill Frank* writes that it is tempting to dismiss an ancient philosopher as "irrelevant for our times," given the scale and complexity of modern states. But Frank argues that to do so would be a mistake.[2] She also says that it would be unwise to dismiss Aristotle on the grounds of his "politics of exclusion." By this, she means Aristotle's apparent advocacy of inequality between women and men or "masters" and "slaves." It is important to look carefully at what Aristotle actually says, she writes, as

> ❝ If we have reasons to want more wealth, we have to
> ask: what precisely are these reasons, how do they work,
> on what are they contingent, and what are the things we
> can "do" with more wealth? ... Income and wealth are
> [not] desirable for their own sake, but because, typically,
> they are admirable general-purpose means for having
> more freedom to lead the kind of lives we have reason
> to value. ❞
> Amartya Sen, *Development as Freedom*

a "closer look opens possibilities [for modern readers] that he is usually seen to be foreclosing." She points out that there has been increasing interest in Aristotle as a source of political insight since the latter half of the twentieth century: "Scholars with varying and often opposing political commitments claim that Aristotle's writings offer rich resources for contemporary politics." [3]

Some, like Strauss, claim that Aristotle offers a justification for a politics based on rule by the "best." Others, such as Frank's colleague, the American philosopher Martha Nussbaum,* argue that Aristotle's focus on education provides "the basis for a well-functioning liberal or social democratic regime."[4] Aristotle is seen as a source of timeless political insight, even between those who may disagree about other things.

Interaction

Aristotle's work inspired Martha Nussbaum's view of virtue ethics.* In turn, virtue ethics stimulated a powerful theory of economic development: the "capability approach."

Championed by the Nobel Prize*-winning Indian economist Amartya Sen,* the Capability Approach states that final aim of development should be "a process of expanding the real freedoms that people enjoy."[5] Sen means that development should not simply make a country richer. Countries can be rich but also restrict their citizens' freedoms, giving them no access to political participation, healthcare, or nutrition. The Capability Approach says the goal of economic development should be to improve the lives of the people who experience that development.

This theory challenged an existing concept of development. In 1990, the British economist John Williamson* wrote an essay called, "What Washington Means By Policy Reform." In it he detailed 10 policy instruments that America used to set policy conditions when giving aid to developing countries.[6] These included:

- Market liberalization
- Increased spending in health and education
- Deficit reduction

These policies, which focused on "the standard economic objectives of growth, low inflation, a visible balance of payments, and an equitable income distribution," became known as the Washington Consensus.* This approach to economics prioritizes economic performance without articulating what that economic performance is *for*, other than the basic preservation of life.[7] That stands in clear contrast to the capability approach, which saw economic performance as a means of developing a country's citizens.

The United Nations Development Program (UNDP)* now uses the capability approach to economics. Instead of emphasizing the Gross National Product (GNP)* of a developing country, it looks at its Human Development Index (HDI).* This measures a combination of the adult literacy rate, average lifespan, and GNP per capita.[8] In other words, Aristotle inspired a concept that now lies at the heart of economic development.

The Continuing Debate

The Capability Approach has been criticized. Some thinkers have emphasized that it is problematic to assume that everyone desires certain universal freedoms, regardless of cultural context.

Although the British academic David Clark* supports the capability approach,* he takes issue with the way it is supposed to work. He asks, for example, which capabilities should the capability approach foster? His argument is that Sen's ideas are too open-ended since he has avoided detailing an objective list of the capabilities that development should bring.

In contrast, the American philosopher Martha Nussbaum,* who specifies a list based on Aristotelian virtue, may be problematic in a different way—her approach may be too high-handed. "Perhaps the only reasonable way of arriving at such a list is to consult the poor themselves," Clark writes. His point is that if we do not, we will have an idea of development that is supposed to be universal, but is in fact based on Western ideas of what it means to live a good life.[9]

Clark provides an example. A survey of South Africans indicated that their concept of the good life involves "jobs, housing, education, income, family and friends, religion, health, good clothes, recreation and relaxation, [and] safety and economic security."[10] Nussbaum, on the other hand, had proposed, "health; bodily health; bodily integrity; senses, imagination, and thought; emotions; practical reason;* affiliation; other species; play; control over one's environment, both political and material."[11]

The South African interviewees' list is more about work and relationships, whereas Nussbaum's focuses more on the development of the self.

NOTES

1   Leo Strauss, *The City and Man* (Chicago: University of Chicago Press, 1964), 21.

2   Jill Frank, *A Democracy of Distinction: Aristotle and the Work of Politics*
    (Chicago: University of Chicago Press, 2005), 4.

3   Frank, *A Democracy of Distinction*, 4.

4   Frank, *A Democracy of Distinction*, 5–6.

5   Amartya Sen, *Development as Freedom* (New York: Alfred A. Knopf, 1999), 3.

6   John Williamson, *Latin American Adjustment: How Much Has Happened?*
    Accessed March 1, 2014 http://faculty.washington.edu/acs22/SinklerSite/
    PS%20322/What%20Washington%20Means%20by%20Policy%20Reform.pdf.

7   Williamson, *Latin American Adjustment*, March 1 2014.

8   United Nations, "Human Development Reports," Accessed Feb 25, 2014,
    http://hdr.undp.org/en/statistics/hdi.

9   David Clark, *Visions of Development: A Study of Human Values*
    (Cheltenham: Edward Elgar, 2002), 27.

10 David Clark, "Capability Approach," in *The Elgar Companion to Development
    Studies* ed. David Clark (Cheltenham: Edward Elgar Publishing Limited,
    2006), 38.

11 Martha Nussbaum, *Women and Human Development: The Capabilities
    Approach* (Cambridge: Cambridge University Press, 2000), 78–80.

MODULE 12
WHERE NEXT?

KEY POINTS

- Aristotle's overall project—to provide an account of politics centered on human improvement—continues to be an important approach.
- The American political philosopher Michael Sandel* applies Aristotle's method to the debate on same-sex marriage, saying that we should legislate according to the virtues that ought to be encouraged.
- Aristotle's *Politics* has inspired thinkers since the Middle Ages* and continues to do so.

Potential

The ideas that Aristotle expressed in his work *Politics* have not only inspired the capability approach to economic development, but also other thinkers who have attempted to apply his political thinking to the modern world.

The American academic Fred D. Miller Jr.,* for example, has argued that modern statesmen should "keep in view Aristotle's suggestions for practical politics."[1] In other words, politicians should keep Aristotle's idea of the "mixed" constitution in mind if we are to avoid pure populist* democracy and oligarchy.

With an echo of Aristotle, he points out that even if modern states distribute political rights among all citizens, economic power tends to concentrate in the hands of the few. Although modern states enjoy a "political order ... subject to representative democratic rule ... economic order is largely the result of decisions by [a few individuals with economic power]."[2]

" The virtues are attracting increasing interest in contemporary philosophical debate. From many different sides one hears of a dissatisfaction with ethical theories that are remote from concrete human experience. "
Martha Nussbaum, "Non-Relative Virtues: An Aristotelian Approach"

Other thinkers, among them the American philosopher Martha Nussbaum,* highlight other aspects of *Politics* that remain relevant today. The idea of the ultimate aim of political association—the achievement of happiness through political structures—would be one.

Aristotle's book remains a source of inspiration for political thinkers from across the political spectrum. His ideas resonate particularly with those who emphasize balance, stability, and human development.

Future Directions

The American political philosopher Michael Sandel has updated Aristotle's ideas for the modern world. Describing his Aristotelian vision of justice in politics, he writes that "justice has something to do honoring, recognizing, promoting, and cultivating virtues and goods implicit in social practices."[3]

Like Aristotle, he argues that if we are to define something, it is vital to understand the ultimate purpose of the thing being described. So to define "rights," it's vital to know exactly what those rights are for. Another key Aristotelian aspect of Sandel's philosophy is that "justice is honorific." To create laws and administer justice, people need to understand "what virtues the social practice should honor and reward."[4] Sandel restates Aristotle's example of the distribution of flutes among flute players. The best flute players should get the best flutes, since "the purpose of flutes is to produce excellent music."[5]

In another example, Sandel addresses the debate over same-sex marriage. Some thinkers say that, in this instance, a principle of non-discrimination should apply to marriage generally. Taken to its logical extreme, however, would this not endorse marriage between any two entities—between members of the same immediate family or between people and objects? Sandel resolves this by arguing that we should ask, "Which interpretation of marriage celebrates virtues worth honoring?"

He cites the decision in favor of same-sex marriage by the South-African born Justice Margaret Marshall,* who argued that disallowing same-sex marriage "confers an official stamp of approval" on destructive stereotypes about same-sex marriage, when they are in fact worthy of the same official respect as heterosexual relationships.[6]

Sandel, in other words, shows that Aristotelian reasoning can help to solve seemingly intractable debates in modern society. The key is to ask what rights or privileges we are trying to distribute, and why.

Summary

Aristotle's *Politics* was dazzlingly original. Moreover, as an early work of empirical* analysis, it was groundbreaking. And it contains a wealth of reflections, distinctions, principles, and concepts that still have significance for political theory today. These include the notion of what constitutes "a good life" and the debate about how much the state should be involved in providing for its citizens.

Although *Politics* was overlooked for some time in the ancient world, its reappraisal by thinkers in the Middle Ages* secured its place in the history of political thought. And, in recent decades, its popularity has increased. Aristotelian ideas have inspired modern scholars like the American political philosopher Michael Sandel, the Indian economist Amartya Sen, and the American philosopher Martha Nussbaum. These thinkers question how society should function in order to provide the best possible lives for their citizens. Their work has ensured that the *Politics* will remain current.

For students of the history of political thought, the book remains enormously important as both a work of political theory and an historical account of the political climate of Ancient Greece. Most important, however, *Politics* is the book that won Aristotle his title as the world's first political scientist.

NOTES

1 Fred D. Miller Jr., "Aristotelian Statecraft and Modern Politics," *Aristotle's Politics Today*, ed. Lenn E. Goodman and Robert B. Talisse (Albany: State University of New York Press, 2008), 30.

2 Miller, "Aristotelian Statecraft and Modern Politics," 30.

3 Michael Sandel, "Justice: What's the Right Thing to Do?" *Boston University Law Review* 91 (2011): 1303.

4 Sandel, "Justice: What's the Right Thing to Do?" 1303.

5 Sandel, "Justice: What's the Right Thing to Do?" 1304.

6 Sandel, "Justice: What's the Right Thing to Do?" 1307–1309.

GLOSSARY

GLOSSARY OF TERMS

Academy (387–86 B.C.E.**):** an elite club of scholars and young Athenian notables founded by Plato.

Aristocracy: literally, "rule by the best": government by a small number of people who merit the position and will, therefore, according to Aristotle, rule without being over-concerned with matters such as wealth.

Callipolis: name given to the "perfect" city in Plato's *Republic*. Its English translation is roughly "Beautiful City."

Capability Approach: theory of economic development that holds that we should define successful economic development by the degree to which individuals are enabled to do what they have reason to want to do.

Classical Era (510–323 B.C.E.**):** period in Greek History that saw the flowering of art, culture, and philosophy for which Ancient Greece is now famous.

Consequentialism: theoretical approach to ethics according to which an action should be judged "right" or "wrong" according to the consequences of that action.

Constitution: for Aristotle, the laws determining who holds power within a society.

Democracy: literally, "rule by the people"; for Aristotle, democracy was undesirable, since the masses would rule in their own interests—over-taxing the wealthy, for example, at the expense of a cohesive society.

Deontology: theoretical approach to ethics according to which the morality of action should be judged based on whether or not it is performed in adherence to rules or out of duty.

Distributive justice: the "just" distribution of goods in a society.

Early Modern: usually held to be the period between the end of the Middle Ages and the beginning of industrialization, around the late fifteenth century to the mid-eighteenth century.

Empiricism: theory that all knowledge is based entirely on sensed evidence as opposed to pure reason.

Ethics: moral principles that govern human behavior with regard to one another.

Eudaemonia: Greek word that means good ("eu") spirit ("daimon"); often thought of as meaning "happiness," the term is better understood to signify the idea of "human flourishing."

Faction: small group of people inside a larger community.

Factionalism: the split into "factions" (self-interested groups) of a community or society, often used with connotations of disagreement and friction.

French Revolution (1789–99): decade of intense political upheaval in France, in which revolutionaries experimented with a variety of different regimes—including a constitutional monarchy, a revolutionary dictatorship, a popular direct democracy, and a liberal republic—before ending with the military dictatorship of Napoleon Bonaparte.

Gross National Product (GNP): the combined value of everything, including goods and services, that citizens of a country produce—even outside that country's borders.

Hellenistic Age: period during which Ancient Greek cultural influence was at its peak, usually held to be the time between the death of Alexander the Great* in 323 B.C.E. and the emergence of the Roman Empire.

Hellenistic Empire (359–323 B.C.E.**)**: group of Greek city-states that Philip II of Macedon brought under his direct control starting in 359 B.C.E. In 333 B.C.E., his son Alexander extended the empire eastward to modern-day India. Upon his death in 323 B.C.E., the empire splintered among his heirs.

Human Development Index (HDI): composite index that shows a country's overall state of "human development" by presenting life expectancy, education, and wealth as a single number.

Humanism: a Renaissance cultural movement that emphasized study of classical literature.

Liberalism: political philosophy founded on ideas about individual freedom and equality.

The Lyceum School: school established by Aristotle in an area of Athens where people would meet called the Lyceum.

Middle Ages: period of European history that starts with the fall of Rome and ends with the Italian Renaissance (roughly from the fifth to the fifteenth century).

Monarchy: a form of government where supremacy lies with a single, usually hereditary, figure, such as a king or queen.

Nobel Prize: international award that recognizes achievement in many academic fields as well as the promotion of world peace. It is often considered one of the highest honors in the world.

Oligarchy: literally, "rule by the few." For Aristotle, an oligarchy was government by a small number of rich men—a poor system of government, since they would govern in their own interests and disregard the poor at the expense of social cohesion.

Olympians: the gods of ancient Greece. The gods were anthropomorphic (meaning they looked and acted like humans) and often manifested parts of nature (such as Zeus, the god of thunder) or society (Hera, the goddess of marriage).

Philosopher King: Plato's idea of the ideal ruler for his ideal state. Only philosophers may truly understand justice, and so must apply their understanding to rule.

***Polis* (plural *polites*):** term in ancient Greece for city-state. The *polis* was usually ruled by their citizen bodies (that is, organized according to a specific constitution).*

Political Naturalism: theory that human political associations are natural rather than (as it is commonly believed) people living "away" from nature.

Polity: rule by the citizens; for Aristotle, the best form of constitutional government.

Populist: a person who seeks to appeal to many masses of people, often used negatively.

Practical Reason (*phronesis*): connection of reasoning to action (instead of pure theorizing, which is unconnected to action). Philosophers who emphasize *phronesis* will think of what is right *in the real world*; philosophers who do not will theorize purely in the abstract.

Pre-Socratic Philosophy: schools of philosophical thought in or near Ancient Greece that were not influenced by Socrates. They focused on explaining the substance of the natural world.

Rhetoric: the art and theory of persuasive language, either written or spoken.

Scholasticism: school of thought that originated in medieval universities and religious institutions. This method examined sources of wisdom (philosophers, theologians, the Bible, and so on) to uncover the knowledge they offered.

Soviet Union: organization of communist states in Eastern Europe and Southeast and Central Asia. It was founded in 1922 and dissolved with the end of the Cold War in 1991.

Teleology: an understanding of historical events, actions, or objects founded on the idea that they exist for their purpose rather than their cause or the forces that brought them into being.

Theology: systematic, academic study of religious principles.

Tyranny: rule by a single individual, acting in his own interests, at the expense of a stable society.

United Nations Development Program (UNDP): formed in 1965, an executive board in the United Nations System dedicated to reducing poverty with a number of broader human-development goals, including the promotion global health, literacy, and democracy.

Utopia: a paradise or otherwise perfect situation—usually an impossibly perfect place.

Virtue Ethics: approach to ethics that emphasizes how one acts, as opposed to the rules one follows ("deontology") or the consequences of one's actions ("consequentialism").

Virtue: in the way Aristotle uses the term, "virtue" refers to excellence of character and proper management of one's impulses. (Eating moderately is virtuous, for example, because it requires the correct regulation of one's body.)

Washington Consensus: term coined by the economist John Williamson* to describe 10 policy prescriptions common to a reform package imposed on developing countries by financial institutions based in Washington DC and promoted by the American government. The policies emphasize macroeconomic stabilization, economic liberalization, and deficit reduction.

Zoology: scientific study of animals.

PEOPLE MENTIONED IN THE TEXT

Alexander III of Macedon (commonly 'the Great') (356–323 B.C.E.) was king of Macedonia who built on his father's conquests in Europe, expanding the empire through Africa and Asia before his death in Babylon.

Andronicus of Rhodes (c. 60 B.C.E.**)** was head of the Lyceum after Aristotle. He published a new edition of Aristotle's work, as well as commentaries on *Physics*, *Ethics*, and *Categories*.

Gertrude Elizabeth Margaret (G. E. M.) Anscombe (1919– 2001) was a British philosopher, born in Ireland. Her work on virtue ethics, especially "Modern Moral Philosophy," is considered foundational for the discipline.

St. Thomas Aquinas (1225–74) was an Italian intellectual and saint who advocated "natural theology," which attempts to prove the existence of God by reasoning from nature.

Ryan Balot is a political philosopher at the University of Toronto in Canada. He is interested in how ancient philosophy can inform modern democracy.

Ernest Barker (1874–1960) was an English academic, primarily concerned with ancient political thought. His reinterpretation of classical philosophy for a modern context has made him one of the most important British thinkers in this vein of the twentieth century.

Edmund Burke (1729–97) was Irish statesman and political thinker who spent most of his career as a parliamentarian in England. He wrote on many topics, including a famously critical response to the French Revolution.

J. H. Burns was a Scottish philosopher of the history of ideas who spent most of his career at University College London. He focused on a range of topics, from medieval political philosophy to procedural issues in democracies.

Paul Cartledge (b. 1947) is a British historian who specializes in Greek culture. He is especially expert in the history and culture of ancient Sparta.

Thomas Case (1844–1925) was a British academic, and fellow of Magdalen College Oxford in moral philosophy.

David Clark is a lecturer in development studies at the University of Cambridge, specializing in notions of human development and cultural issues.

Pierre Destrée is a professor of ancient history and philosophy at the University of Louvain in Belgium. He specializes in Plato and Aristotle.

Stephen Everson is a lecturer in philosophy of mind at the University of York in the United Kingdom.

Jill Frank is an academic at the University of South Carolina in the United States. She specializes in classical political theory.

Dorothea Frede (b. 1941) is a professor of philosophy at the University of California, Berkeley. She is a notable commentator on Aristotle's *Ethics*.

Thomas Hobbes (1588–1679) was an English political philosopher. He is famous for his argument that political order is artificial, and that life in nature is "poor, nasty, brutish, and short."

Werner Jaeger (1888–1961) was a German classicist famous for linking the thought of Plato and Aristotle. He wrote that Aristotle is the practical application of Plato.

David C. Lindberg (1935–2015) was an American philosopher of science, especially the history of science in the medieval and renaissance worlds. In 1999, he received the Sarton Medal (the highest award) from the History of Science Society.

Anthony Arthur (A. A.) Long (b. 1937) is a British classical scholar at the University of California at Berkeley.

Carnes Lord (b. 1944) is a professor of strategic leadership at the US Naval War College. He is interested in different approaches to political authority throughout history.

Niccolò Machiavelli (1469–1527) was an Italian diplomat (from Florence), political thinker, and statesman. His work *The Prince* is considered to the first work of modern political theory.

Margaret Marshall (b. 1944) is a South African-born lawyer and judge. She served as the first woman on the Massachusetts Supreme Judicial Court.

Fred D. Miller, Jr. is an emeritus professor of philosophy at Bowling Green University who specializes in Aristotle.

Martha Nussbaum (b. 1947) is an American philosopher who specializes in virtue ethics and is one of the major figures in the renewed twentieth century interest in Aristotle. She is especially interested in including feminism in virtue ethics and development.

Stefano Perfetti is a professor of medieval and ancient history at the University of Pisa, specializing in the impact of Aristotle.

Petrarch (Francisco Petrarca) (1304–74) was an Italian scholar and poet. He is partially responsible for finding and popularizing Cicero's ancient work throughout Renaissance Europe.

Philip II of Macedon (382–336 B.C.E.**)** was the king of Macedonia (a region to the north of present-day Greece) and led the Macedonian conquest of Greece. He was assassinated after he united much of Greece and began invading Persia.

Plato (428–348 B.C.E.**)** was an ancient Greek philosopher and perhaps the most important philosopher in Western history. His philosophy spanned many issues—from justice, to love, to the metaphysical—and defined the approach of all who followed him for centuries.

Michael Sandel (b. 1953) is an American political philosopher. He is most famous as a theorist of justice and community.

Malcolm Schofield is a professor of classics at the University of Cambridge, specializing in ancient political thought.

Amartya Sen (b. 1933) is an Indian Economist and Nobel laureate. (He was awarded the Nobel Prize in 1998 for his work on welfare economics). He teaches at the Universities of Cambridge and Oxford, as well as Harvard University.

Socrates (470–399 B.C.E.**)** was an ancient Greek philosopher. He never published work of his own, but those around him, especially Plato, widely reported on his ideas. His work laid the foundations of Western philosophy.

Leo Strauss (1899–1973) was a German American political philosopher, specializing in the history of classical philosophy. He is especially prominent among conservative thinkers, trying to extract timeless wisdom from "great books."

Theophrastus (371–287 B.C.E.**)** was the successor to Aristotle as head of the Lyceum. He is most famous for his work on classifying plants.

William of Moerbeke (1215/35–1286) was a Flemish medieval translator and philosopher, especially well known for translating medical and scientific texts into Latin (a language most educated people spoke at the time) from Greek (a language fewer people spoke).

John Williamson (b. 1937) is an English economist and international statesman famous for coining the term "Washington Consensus" to describe the pro-free market policy mix promoted by international financial institutions in the 1980s. He has worked with the United Nations, World Bank, and International Monetary Fund in advisory capacities.

Xenophanes (570–475 B.C.E.**)** was a pre-Socratic Greek philosopher and satirist. He was famously critical of closely held Greek beliefs, including reverence for the gods and athletic conquest.

WORKS CITED

WORKS CITED

Anscombe, G.E.M. "Modern Moral Philosophy." *Philosophy* 33, No. 124 (1958): 1–19.

Aquinas, St. Thomas. *Commentary on Aristotle's Politics*, translated by Richard J. Regan. Indianapolis: Hackett, 2007.

_____, *Summa Theologica*, (Mobilereference: 2010).

Aristotle, *History of the Animals*. Adelaide: University of Adelaide. ebook. https://ebooks.adelaide.edu.au/a/aristotle/history/book1.html.

_____. *Physics*. Translated by Robin Waterfield. Oxford: Oxford World's Classics, 2008.

_____. "Nicomachean Ethics: Book X, Chapter 9" in *The Politics and The Constitution of Athens*, edited by Stephen Everson of *Cambridge Texts in the History of Political Thought*, series editors Raymond Geuss and Quentin Skinner. Cambridge: Cambridge University Press, 1996.

_____. *Poetics*. Translated by Richard Janko. Indianapolis: Hackett Publishing, 1987.

_____. *Politics* in *The Politics and The Constitution of Athens*, edited by Stephen Everson of *Cambridge Texts in the History of Political Thought*, series editors Raymond Geuss and Quentin Skinner. Cambridge: Cambridge University Press, 1996.

Balot, Ryan. *Greek Political Thought*. Oxford: Blackwell, 2006.

Barker, Sir Ernest. *The Political Thought of Plato and Aristotle*. New York: Dover Publications, 1959.

Blackson, Thomas. *Ancient Greek Philosophy*. Chichester: Wiley-Blackwell, 2011.

Burke, Edmund. *Reflections on the Revolution in France*. New Haven: Yale University Press, 2003.

J.H. Burns. "Introduction: Politics, Institutions, and Ideas," in *The Cambridge History of Medieval Political Thought.* Cambridge: Cambridge University Press, 1988.

Cartledge, Paul. "Greek Political Thought: The Historical Context." In *The Cambridge History of Greek and Roman Political Thought*, edited by Christopher Rowe et al. Cambridge: Cambridge University Press, 2000.

Case, Thomas. "Aristotle." In *Aristotle's Philosophical Development: Problems and Prospects*, edited by William Robert Wians. London: Rowman and Littlefield, 1990.

Clark, David. *Visions of Development: A Study of Human Values*. Cheltenham: Edward Elgar, 2002.

_____, "Capability Approach." In *The Elgar Companion to Development Studies*, edited by David Clark. Cheltenham: Edward Elgar Publishing Limited, 2006.

Destrée, Pierre. "Education, Leisure and Politics." In *The Cambridge Companion to* Aristotle's *Politics*, edited by Marguerite Deslauriers and Pierre Destrée. Cambridge and New York: Cambridge University Press, 2013.

Everson, Stephen, "Introduction." *The Politics and The Constitution of Athens*, edited by Stephen Everson. In *Cambridge Texts in the History of Political Thought*, series editors Raymond Geuss and Quentin Skinner. Cambridge: Cambridge University Press, 1996.

Frank, Jill. *A Democracy of Distinction: Aristotle and the Work of Politics*. Chicago: University of Chicago Press, 2005.

Frede, Dorothea. "The Political Character of Aristotle's Ethics." In *The Cambridge Companion to Aristotle's Politics*. Cambridge: Cambridge University Press, 2013. .

Graham, Daniel. *Aristotle's Two Systems*. Oxford: Oxford University Press, 1990.

Hobbes, Thomas. *Leviathan*. Edited by J.C.A. Gaskin. Oxford: Oxford University Press, 1998.

Hursthouse, Rosalind. *On Virtue Ethics*. Oxford: Oxford University Press, 1999.

Jaeger, Werner. *Aristotle: Fundamentals of the History of His Development*. Translated by Richard Robinson. Oxford: Oxford University Press, 1948.

Kleinhenz, Christopher. *Medieval Italy: An Encyclopedia Volume I A-K*. Oxford: Routledge, 2004.

Lindberg, David C. *The Beginnings of Western Science: The European Scientific Tradition in Philosophical, Religious, and Institutional Context, Prehistory to AD 1450*. Chicago: University of Chicago, 2008.

Long, A.A. "The Scope of Early Greek Philosophy." In *The Cambridge Companion to Early Greek Philosophy*. Cambridge: Cambridge University Press, 1999.

Lord, Carnes. "The Character and Composition of Aristotle's *Politics*." *Political Theory* 9, No. 4 (1981): 459-478.

Lynch, John Patrick. *Aristotle's School: A Study of a Greek Educational Institution*. Berkeley: University of California Press, 1972.

Machiavelli, Niccolò. *The Prince*. Edited by Quentin Skinner and Russell Price. Cambridge: Cambridge University Press, 1988.

Martin, Conor. "Some Medieval Commentaries on Aristotle's *Politics*." *History* 36 (1951) 126-127: 29-44.

Miller, Fred D. "Aristotelian Statecraft and Modern Politics." In *Aristotle's Politics Today*. Edited by Lenn E. Goodman and Robert B. Talisse. Albany: State University of New York Press, 2008.

Natali, Carlo. *Aristotle: His Life and School*. Princeton: Princeton University Press, 2013.

Nussbaum, Martha. "Non-Relative Virtues: An Aristotelian Approach." *Midwest Studies in Philosophy 13*. No. 1 (1988): 32-53.

_____. *Women and Human Development: The Capabilities Approach*. Cambridge: Cambridge University Press, 2000.

Perfetti, Stefano. *Aristotle's Zoology and its Renaissance Commentators.* Leuven: Leuven University Press, 2000.

Plato, *The Republic*. Edited by G.R.F. Ferrarri. In *Cambridge Texts in the History of Political Thought,* series editors Raymond Geuss and Quentin Skinner. Cambridge: Cambridge University Press, 2003.

_____. Plato, *Gorgias*, translated by Robin Waterfield. Oxford: Oxford World's Classics, 1995.

Sacks, David. "Xenophanes." In *A Dictionary of the Ancient Greek World*. Oxford: Oxford University Press, 1995.

Sandel, Michael. "Justice: What's the Right Thing to Do?" *Boston University Law Review* 91 (2011): 1301-1569.

Schofield, Malcolm. "Aristotle: An Introduction," In *The Cambridge History of Greek and Roman Political Thought,* edited by Christopher Rowe et al. Cambridge: Cambridge University Press, 2000.

_____. "Ideology and Philosophy in Aristotle's Theory of Slavery." In *Aristotle's Politics: Critical Essays*, edited by Richard Kraut and Steven Skultety. Lanham: Rowman and Littlefield, 2005.

Sen, Amartya. *Development as Freedom*. New York: Alfred A. Knopf, 1999.

Strauss, Leo *The City and Man*. Chicago: University of Chicago Press, 1964.

United Nations, "Human Development Reports." Accessed Feb 25, 2014, http://hdr.undp.org/en/statistics/hdi.

Williamson, John. "What Washington means by Policy Reform," in *Latin American Adjustment: How Much Has Happened?* edited by John Williamson. Washington: Institute for International Economics, March 1990. Accessed July 19, 2015, http://www.iie.com/publications/papers/paper.cfm?researchid=486.

THE MACAT LIBRARY
BY DISCIPLINE

AFRICANA STUDIES

Chinua Achebe's *An Image of Africa: Racism in Conrad's Heart of Darkness*
W. E. B. Du Bois's *The Souls of Black Folk*
Zora Neale Huston's *Characteristics of Negro Expression*
Martin Luther King Jr's *Why We Can't Wait*
Toni Morrison's *Playing in the Dark: Whiteness in the American Literary Imagination*

ANTHROPOLOGY

Arjun Appadurai's *Modernity at Large: Cultural Dimensions of Globalisation*
Philippe Ariès's *Centuries of Childhood*
Franz Boas's *Race, Language and Culture*
Kim Chan & Renée Mauborgne's *Blue Ocean Strategy*
Jared Diamond's *Guns, Germs & Steel: the Fate of Human Societies*
Jared Diamond's *Collapse: How Societies Choose to Fail or Survive*
E. E. Evans-Pritchard's *Witchcraft, Oracles and Magic Among the Azande*
James Ferguson's *The Anti-Politics Machine*
Clifford Geertz's *The Interpretation of Cultures*
David Graeber's *Debt: the First 5000 Years*
Karen Ho's *Liquidated: An Ethnography of Wall Street*
Geert Hofstede's *Culture's Consequences: Comparing Values, Behaviors, Institutes and Organizations across Nations*
Claude Lévi-Strauss's *Structural Anthropology*
Jay Macleod's *Ain't No Makin' It: Aspirations and Attainment in a Low-Income Neighborhood*
Saba Mahmood's *The Politics of Piety: The Islamic Revival and the Feminist Subject*
Marcel Mauss's *The Gift*

BUSINESS

Jean Lave & Etienne Wenger's *Situated Learning*
Theodore Levitt's *Marketing Myopia*
Burton G. Malkiel's *A Random Walk Down Wall Street*
Douglas McGregor's *The Human Side of Enterprise*
Michael Porter's *Competitive Strategy: Creating and Sustaining Superior Performance*
John Kotter's *Leading Change*
C. K. Prahalad & Gary Hamel's *The Core Competence of the Corporation*

CRIMINOLOGY

Michelle Alexander's *The New Jim Crow: Mass Incarceration in the Age of Colorblindness*
Michael R. Gottfredson & Travis Hirschi's *A General Theory of Crime*
Richard Herrnstein & Charles A. Murray's *The Bell Curve: Intelligence and Class Structure in American Life*
Elizabeth Loftus's *Eyewitness Testimony*
Jay Macleod's *Ain't No Makin' It: Aspirations and Attainment in a Low-Income Neighborhood*
Philip Zimbardo's *The Lucifer Effect*

ECONOMICS

Janet Abu-Lughod's *Before European Hegemony*
Ha-Joon Chang's *Kicking Away the Ladder*
David Brion Davis's *The Problem of Slavery in the Age of Revolution*
Milton Friedman's *The Role of Monetary Policy*
Milton Friedman's *Capitalism and Freedom*
David Graeber's *Debt: the First 5000 Years*
Friedrich Hayek's *The Road to Serfdom*
Karen Ho's *Liquidated: An Ethnography of Wall Street*

John Maynard Keynes's *The General Theory of Employment, Interest and Money*
Charles P. Kindleberger's *Manias, Panics and Crashes*
Robert Lucas's *Why Doesn't Capital Flow from Rich to Poor Countries?*
Burton G. Malkiel's *A Random Walk Down Wall Street*
Thomas Robert Malthus's *An Essay on the Principle of Population*
Karl Marx's *Capital*
Thomas Piketty's *Capital in the Twenty-First Century*
Amartya Sen's *Development as Freedom*
Adam Smith's *The Wealth of Nations*
Nassim Nicholas Taleb's *The Black Swan: The Impact of the Highly Improbable*
Amos Tversky's & Daniel Kahneman's *Judgment under Uncertainty: Heuristics and Biases*
Mahbub Ul Haq's *Reflections on Human Development*
Max Weber's *The Protestant Ethic and the Spirit of Capitalism*

FEMINISM AND GENDER STUDIES

Judith Butler's *Gender Trouble*
Simone De Beauvoir's *The Second Sex*
Michel Foucault's *History of Sexuality*
Betty Friedan's *The Feminine Mystique*
Saba Mahmood's *The Politics of Piety: The Islamic Revival and the Feminist Subject*
Joan Wallach Scott's *Gender and the Politics of History*
Mary Wollstonecraft's *A Vindication of the Rights of Woman*
Virginia Woolf's *A Room of One's Own*

GEOGRAPHY

The Brundtland Report's *Our Common Future*
Rachel Carson's *Silent Spring*
Charles Darwin's *On the Origin of Species*
James Ferguson's *The Anti-Politics Machine*
Jane Jacobs's *The Death and Life of Great American Cities*
James Lovelock's *Gaia: A New Look at Life on Earth*
Amartya Sen's *Development as Freedom*
Mathis Wackernagel & William Rees's *Our Ecological Footprint*

HISTORY

Janet Abu-Lughod's *Before European Hegemony*
Benedict Anderson's *Imagined Communities*
Bernard Bailyn's *The Ideological Origins of the American Revolution*
Hanna Batatu's *The Old Social Classes And The Revolutionary Movements Of Iraq*
Christopher Browning's *Ordinary Men: Reserve Police Batallion 101 and the Final Solution in Poland*
Edmund Burke's *Reflections on the Revolution in France*
William Cronon's *Nature's Metropolis: Chicago And The Great West*
Alfred W. Crosby's *The Columbian Exchange*
Hamid Dabashi's *Iran: A People Interrupted*
David Brion Davis's *The Problem of Slavery in the Age of Revolution*
Nathalie Zemon Davis's *The Return of Martin Guerre*
Jared Diamond's *Guns, Germs & Steel: the Fate of Human Societies*
Frank Dikotter's *Mao's Great Famine*
John W Dower's *War Without Mercy: Race And Power In The Pacific War*
W. E. B. Du Bois's *The Souls of Black Folk*
Richard J. Evans's *In Defence of History*
Lucien Febvre's *The Problem of Unbelief in the 16th Century*
Sheila Fitzpatrick's *Everyday Stalinism*

Eric Foner's *Reconstruction: America's Unfinished Revolution, 1863-1877*
Michel Foucault's *Discipline and Punish*
Michel Foucault's *History of Sexuality*
Francis Fukuyama's *The End of History and the Last Man*
John Lewis Gaddis's *We Now Know: Rethinking Cold War History*
Ernest Gellner's *Nations and Nationalism*
Eugene Genovese's *Roll, Jordan, Roll: The World the Slaves Made*
Carlo Ginzburg's *The Night Battles*
Daniel Goldhagen's *Hitler's Willing Executioners*
Jack Goldstone's *Revolution and Rebellion in the Early Modern World*
Antonio Gramsci's *The Prison Notebooks*
Alexander Hamilton, John Jay & James Madison's *The Federalist Papers*
Christopher Hill's *The World Turned Upside Down*
Carole Hillenbrand's *The Crusades: Islamic Perspectives*
Thomas Hobbes's *Leviathan*
Eric Hobsbawm's *The Age Of Revolution*
John A. Hobson's *Imperialism: A Study*
Albert Hourani's *History of the Arab Peoples*
Samuel P. Huntington's *The Clash of Civilizations and the Remaking of World Order*
C. L. R. James's *The Black Jacobins*
Tony Judt's *Postwar: A History of Europe Since 1945*
Ernst Kantorowicz's *The King's Two Bodies: A Study in Medieval Political Theology*
Paul Kennedy's *The Rise and Fall of the Great Powers*
Ian Kershaw's *The "Hitler Myth": Image and Reality in the Third Reich*
John Maynard Keynes's *The General Theory of Employment, Interest and Money*
Charles P. Kindleberger's *Manias, Panics and Crashes*
Martin Luther King Jr's *Why We Can't Wait*
Henry Kissinger's *World Order: Reflections on the Character of Nations and the Course of History*
Thomas Kuhn's *The Structure of Scientific Revolutions*
Georges Lefebvre's *The Coming of the French Revolution*
John Locke's *Two Treatises of Government*
Niccolò Machiavelli's *The Prince*
Thomas Robert Malthus's *An Essay on the Principle of Population*
Mahmood Mamdani's *Citizen and Subject: Contemporary Africa And The Legacy Of Late Colonialism*
Karl Marx's *Capital*
Stanley Milgram's *Obedience to Authority*
John Stuart Mill's *On Liberty*
Thomas Paine's *Common Sense*
Thomas Paine's *Rights of Man*
Geoffrey Parker's *Global Crisis: War, Climate Change and Catastrophe in the Seventeenth Century*
Jonathan Riley-Smith's *The First Crusade and the Idea of Crusading*
Jean-Jacques Rousseau's *The Social Contract*
Joan Wallach Scott's *Gender and the Politics of History*
Theda Skocpol's *States and Social Revolutions*
Adam Smith's *The Wealth of Nations*
Timothy Snyder's *Bloodlands: Europe Between Hitler and Stalin*
Sun Tzu's *The Art of War*
Keith Thomas's *Religion and the Decline of Magic*
Thucydides's *The History of the Peloponnesian War*
Frederick Jackson Turner's *The Significance of the Frontier in American History*
Odd Arne Westad's *The Global Cold War: Third World Interventions And The Making Of Our Times*

LITERATURE

Chinua Achebe's *An Image of Africa: Racism in Conrad's Heart of Darkness*
Roland Barthes's *Mythologies*
Homi K. Bhabha's *The Location of Culture*
Judith Butler's *Gender Trouble*
Simone De Beauvoir's *The Second Sex*
Ferdinand De Saussure's *Course in General Linguistics*
T. S. Eliot's *The Sacred Wood: Essays on Poetry and Criticism*
Zora Neale Huston's *Characteristics of Negro Expression*
Toni Morrison's *Playing in the Dark: Whiteness in the American Literary Imagination*
Edward Said's *Orientalism*
Gayatri Chakravorty Spivak's *Can the Subaltern Speak?*
Mary Wollstonecraft's *A Vindication of the Rights of Women*
Virginia Woolf's *A Room of One's Own*

PHILOSOPHY

Elizabeth Anscombe's *Modern Moral Philosophy*
Hannah Arendt's *The Human Condition*
Aristotle's *Metaphysics*
Aristotle's *Nicomachean Ethics*
Edmund Gettier's *Is Justified True Belief Knowledge?*
Georg Wilhelm Friedrich Hegel's *Phenomenology of Spirit*
David Hume's *Dialogues Concerning Natural Religion*
David Hume's *The Enquiry for Human Understanding*
Immanuel Kant's *Religion within the Boundaries of Mere Reason*
Immanuel Kant's *Critique of Pure Reason*
Søren Kierkegaard's *The Sickness Unto Death*
Søren Kierkegaard's *Fear and Trembling*
C. S. Lewis's *The Abolition of Man*
Alasdair MacIntyre's *After Virtue*
Marcus Aurelius's *Meditations*
Friedrich Nietzsche's *On the Genealogy of Morality*
Friedrich Nietzsche's *Beyond Good and Evil*
Plato's *Republic*
Plato's *Symposium*
Jean-Jacques Rousseau's *The Social Contract*
Gilbert Ryle's *The Concept of Mind*
Baruch Spinoza's *Ethics*
Sun Tzu's *The Art of War*
Ludwig Wittgenstein's *Philosophical Investigations*

POLITICS

Benedict Anderson's *Imagined Communities*
Aristotle's *Politics*
Bernard Bailyn's *The Ideological Origins of the American Revolution*
Edmund Burke's *Reflections on the Revolution in France*
John C. Calhoun's *A Disquisition on Government*
Ha-Joon Chang's *Kicking Away the Ladder*
Hamid Dabashi's *Iran: A People Interrupted*
Hamid Dabashi's *Theology of Discontent: The Ideological Foundation of the Islamic Revolution in Iran*
Robert Dahl's *Democracy and its Critics*
Robert Dahl's *Who Governs?*
David Brion Davis's *The Problem of Slavery in the Age of Revolution*

Alexis De Tocqueville's *Democracy in America*
James Ferguson's *The Anti-Politics Machine*
Frank Dikotter's *Mao's Great Famine*
Sheila Fitzpatrick's *Everyday Stalinism*
Eric Foner's *Reconstruction: America's Unfinished Revolution, 1863-1877*
Milton Friedman's *Capitalism and Freedom*
Francis Fukuyama's *The End of History and the Last Man*
John Lewis Gaddis's *We Now Know: Rethinking Cold War History*
Ernest Gellner's *Nations and Nationalism*
David Graeber's *Debt: the First 5000 Years*
Antonio Gramsci's *The Prison Notebooks*
Alexander Hamilton, John Jay & James Madison's *The Federalist Papers*
Friedrich Hayek's *The Road to Serfdom*
Christopher Hill's *The World Turned Upside Down*
Thomas Hobbes's *Leviathan*
John A. Hobson's *Imperialism: A Study*
Samuel P. Huntington's *The Clash of Civilizations and the Remaking of World Order*
Tony Judt's *Postwar: A History of Europe Since 1945*
David C. Kang's *China Rising: Peace, Power and Order in East Asia*
Paul Kennedy's *The Rise and Fall of Great Powers*
Robert Keohane's *After Hegemony*
Martin Luther King Jr.'s *Why We Can't Wait*
Henry Kissinger's *World Order: Reflections on the Character of Nations and the Course of History*
John Locke's *Two Treatises of Government*
Niccolò Machiavelli's *The Prince*
Thomas Robert Malthus's *An Essay on the Principle of Population*
Mahmood Mamdani's *Citizen and Subject: Contemporary Africa And The Legacy Of Late Colonialism*
Karl Marx's *Capital*
John Stuart Mill's *On Liberty*
John Stuart Mill's *Utilitarianism*
Hans Morgenthau's *Politics Among Nations*
Thomas Paine's *Common Sense*
Thomas Paine's *Rights of Man*
Thomas Piketty's *Capital in the Twenty-First Century*
Robert D. Putman's *Bowling Alone*
John Rawls's *Theory of Justice*
Jean-Jacques Rousseau's *The Social Contract*
Theda Skocpol's *States and Social Revolutions*
Adam Smith's *The Wealth of Nations*
Sun Tzu's *The Art of War*
Henry David Thoreau's *Civil Disobedience*
Thucydides's *The History of the Peloponnesian War*
Kenneth Waltz's *Theory of International Politics*
Max Weber's *Politics as a Vocation*
Odd Arne Westad's *The Global Cold War: Third World Interventions And The Making Of Our Times*

POSTCOLONIAL STUDIES

Roland Barthes's *Mythologies*
Frantz Fanon's *Black Skin, White Masks*
Homi K. Bhabha's *The Location of Culture*
Gustavo Gutiérrez's *A Theology of Liberation*
Edward Said's *Orientalism*
Gayatri Chakravorty Spivak's *Can the Subaltern Speak?*

PSYCHOLOGY

Gordon Allport's *The Nature of Prejudice*
Alan Baddeley & Graham Hitch's *Aggression: A Social Learning Analysis*
Albert Bandura's *Aggression: A Social Learning Analysis*
Leon Festinger's *A Theory of Cognitive Dissonance*
Sigmund Freud's *The Interpretation of Dreams*
Betty Friedan's *The Feminine Mystique*
Michael R. Gottfredson & Travis Hirschi's *A General Theory of Crime*
Eric Hoffer's *The True Believer: Thoughts on the Nature of Mass Movements*
William James's *Principles of Psychology*
Elizabeth Loftus's *Eyewitness Testimony*
A. H. Maslow's *A Theory of Human Motivation*
Stanley Milgram's *Obedience to Authority*
Steven Pinker's *The Better Angels of Our Nature*
Oliver Sacks's *The Man Who Mistook His Wife For a Hat*
Richard Thaler & Cass Sunstein's *Nudge: Improving Decisions About Health, Wealth and Happiness*
Amos Tversky's *Judgment under Uncertainty: Heuristics and Biases*
Philip Zimbardo's *The Lucifer Effect*

SCIENCE

Rachel Carson's *Silent Spring*
William Cronon's *Nature's Metropolis: Chicago And The Great West*
Alfred W. Crosby's *The Columbian Exchange*
Charles Darwin's *On the Origin of Species*
Richard Dawkin's *The Selfish Gene*
Thomas Kuhn's *The Structure of Scientific Revolutions*
Geoffrey Parker's *Global Crisis: War, Climate Change and Catastrophe in the Seventeenth Century*
Mathis Wackernagel & William Rees's *Our Ecological Footprint*

SOCIOLOGY

Michelle Alexander's *The New Jim Crow: Mass Incarceration in the Age of Colorblindness*
Gordon Allport's *The Nature of Prejudice*
Albert Bandura's *Aggression: A Social Learning Analysis*
Hanna Batatu's *The Old Social Classes And The Revolutionary Movements Of Iraq*
Ha-Joon Chang's *Kicking Away the Ladder*
W. E. B. Du Bois's *The Souls of Black Folk*
Émile Durkheim's *On Suicide*
Frantz Fanon's *Black Skin, White Masks*
Frantz Fanon's *The Wretched of the Earth*
Eric Foner's *Reconstruction: America's Unfinished Revolution, 1863-1877*
Eugene Genovese's *Roll, Jordan, Roll: The World the Slaves Made*
Jack Goldstone's *Revolution and Rebellion in the Early Modern World*
Antonio Gramsci's *The Prison Notebooks*
Richard Herrnstein & Charles A Murray's *The Bell Curve: Intelligence and Class Structure in American Life*
Eric Hoffer's *The True Believer: Thoughts on the Nature of Mass Movements*
Jane Jacobs's *The Death and Life of Great American Cities*
Robert Lucas's *Why Doesn't Capital Flow from Rich to Poor Countries?*
Jay Macleod's *Ain't No Makin' It: Aspirations and Attainment in a Low Income Neighborhood*
Elaine May's *Homeward Bound: American Families in the Cold War Era*
Douglas McGregor's *The Human Side of Enterprise*
C. Wright Mills's *The Sociological Imagination*

Thomas Piketty's *Capital in the Twenty-First Century*
Robert D. Putman's *Bowling Alone*
David Riesman's *The Lonely Crowd: A Study of the Changing American Character*
Edward Said's *Orientalism*
Joan Wallach Scott's *Gender and the Politics of History*
Theda Skocpol's *States and Social Revolutions*
Max Weber's *The Protestant Ethic and the Spirit of Capitalism*

THEOLOGY

Augustine's *Confessions*
Benedict's *Rule of St Benedict*
Gustavo Gutiérrez's *A Theology of Liberation*
Carole Hillenbrand's *The Crusades: Islamic Perspectives*
David Hume's *Dialogues Concerning Natural Religion*
Immanuel Kant's *Religion within the Boundaries of Mere Reason*
Ernst Kantorowicz's *The King's Two Bodies: A Study in Medieval Political Theology*
Søren Kierkegaard's *The Sickness Unto Death*
C. S. Lewis's *The Abolition of Man*
Saba Mahmood's *The Politics of Piety: The Islamic Revival and the Feminist Subject*
Baruch Spinoza's *Ethics*
Keith Thomas's *Religion and the Decline of Magic*

COMING SOON

Chris Argyris's *The Individual and the Organisation*
Seyla Benhabib's *The Rights of Others*
Walter Benjamin's *The Work Of Art in the Age of Mechanical Reproduction*
John Berger's *Ways of Seeing*
Pierre Bourdieu's *Outline of a Theory of Practice*
Mary Douglas's *Purity and Danger*
Roland Dworkin's *Taking Rights Seriously*
James G. March's *Exploration and Exploitation in Organisational Learning*
Ikujiro Nonaka's *A Dynamic Theory of Organizational Knowledge Creation*
Griselda Pollock's *Vision and Difference*
Amartya Sen's *Inequality Re-Examined*
Susan Sontag's *On Photography*
Yasser Tabbaa's *The Transformation of Islamic Art*
Ludwig von Mises's *Theory of Money and Credit*

Macat Disciplines

Access the greatest ideas and thinkers across entire disciplines, including

MAN AND THE ENVIRONMENT

The Brundtland Report's, *Our Common Future*
Rachel Carson's, *Silent Spring*
James Lovelock's, *Gaia: A New Look at Life on Earth*
Mathis Wackernagel & William Rees's, *Our Ecological Footprint*

Macat analyses are available from all good bookshops and libraries.

Access hundreds of analyses through one, multimedia tool.
Join free for one month **library.macat.com**

Macat Disciplines

Access the greatest ideas and thinkers across entire disciplines, including

THE FUTURE OF DEMOCRACY

Robert A. Dahl's, *Democracy and Its Critics*
Robert A. Dahl's, *Who Governs?*
Alexis De Toqueville's, *Democracy in America*
Niccolò Machiavelli's, *The Prince*
John Stuart Mill's, *On Liberty*
Robert D. Putnam's, *Bowling Alone*
Jean-Jacques Rousseau's, *The Social Contract*
Henry David Thoreau's, *Civil Disobedience*

Macat Disciplines

Access the greatest ideas and thinkers across entire disciplines, including

TOTALITARIANISM

Sheila Fitzpatrick's, *Everyday Stalinism*
Ian Kershaw's, *The "Hitler Myth"*
Timothy Snyder's, *Bloodlands*

Macat Pairs

Analyse historical and modern issues from opposite sides of an argument. Pairs include:

RACE AND IDENTITY

Zora Neale Hurston's
Characteristics of Negro Expression

Using material collected on anthropological expeditions to the South, Zora Neale Hurston explains how expression in African American culture in the early twentieth century departs from the art of white America. At the time, African American art was often criticized for copying white culture. For Hurston, this criticism misunderstood how art works. European tradition views art as something fixed. But Hurston describes a creative process that is alive, ever-changing, and largely improvisational. She maintains that African American art works through a process called 'mimicry'—where an imitated object or verbal pattern, for example, is reshaped and altered until it becomes something new, novel—and worthy of attention.

Frantz Fanon's
Black Skin, White Masks

Black Skin, White Masks offers a radical analysis of the psychological effects of colonization on the colonized.

Fanon witnessed the effects of colonization first hand both in his birthplace, Martinique, and again later in life when he worked as a psychiatrist in another French colony, Algeria. His text is uncompromising in form and argument. He dissects the dehumanizing effects of colonialism, arguing that it destroys the native sense of identity, forcing people to adapt to an alien set of values—including a core belief that they are inferior. This results in deep psychological trauma.

Fanon's work played a pivotal role in the civil rights movements of the 1960s.

Macat analyses are available from all good bookshops and libraries.

Access hundreds of analyses through one, multimedia tool.
Join free for one month **library.macat.com**

For Product Safety Concerns and Information please contact our EU
representative GPSR@taylorandfrancis.com Taylor & Francis Verlag GmbH,
Kaufingerstraße 24, 80331 München, Germany

Printed and bound by CPI Group (UK) Ltd, Croydon, CR0 4YY
08/06/2025
01896998-0003